Twayne's United States Authors Series

Sylvia E. Bowman, *Editor*

INDIANA UNIVERSITY

Eugene O'Neill

EUGENE O'NEILL

by FREDERIC I. CARPENTER
University of California at Berkeley

TWAYNE PUBLISHERS
A DIVISION OF G. K. HALL & CO., BOSTON

Library of Congress Catalog Card Number: 64-20716
ISBN   0-8057-0572-4

MANUFACTURED IN THE UNITED STATES OF AMERICA

FOR DIXIE
WITH GRATEFUL ACKNOWLEDGMENT TO
LILLIAN COOK CARPENTER, PSYCHOLOGIST

INDIA
36-37

Contents

About the Author

Frederic I. Carpenter is the author of *Emerson and Asia* (1930), *Emerson Handbook* (1953), *American Literature and the Dream* (1955), and *Robinson Jeffers (TUSAS 22*, 1962). He has published many critical articles in scholarly magazines, often on contemporary American writers.

Dr. Carpenter graduated from Harvard in 1924, then did further study at Harvard and the University of Chicago in comparative literature, taking his doctorate at Chicago in 1929. He has taught at the University of Chicago, at Harvard and at the University of California at Berkeley.

Preface

WHEN EUGENE O'NEILL DIED in 1953, he left instructions that he be buried without ceremony, and that the headstone over his grave be inscribed with the single word: "O'Neill." A decade later the most complete biography of him was entitled simply, *O'Neill.* This confident assumption of uniqueness might seem mere egotism were it not completely realistic. Both the man and his dramatic achievement were unique: there was something monolithic about him. But there was also something protean. "O'Neill" was somehow greater than the sum of all his work.

In 1951 the Swiss critic, Heinrich Straumann, expressed this feeling:

> There may be arguments about who is the greatest living American poet, or novelist, or essayist, but the position of O'Neill as the leading American dramatist has never been seriously questioned. This is an almost unique occurrence in modern criticism, and can only be explained by the fact that practically any approach to his art yields results of the first order, which in turn testifies to the wealth in scope, subject material, ideas and dramatic styles in his work.[1]

Mr. Straumann (I take it) did not mean that anyone writing about O'Neill would produce results of the first order: rather, O'Neill possesses a fascination for the biographer and for the philosopher, as well as for the dramatist and the literary critic.

The first chapter of this book relates O'Neill's life to his plays. It is exceptionally long because his biography is exceptionally important to the understanding of his work, and because it is exceptionally interesting. Many of his plays are autobiographical, of course. But beyond biography, his life as a whole has seemed to develop the dramatic stages of a kind of continuing "quest." O'Neill struggled with the problems of his individual life, of his family, and of his times (with what he called "the sickness of today"). And these personal struggles have also seemed to recapitulate the universal problems of man's "long journey" through all times and places. The tragedy of his life is related not only to the dramatic tragedies which he wrote but to the archetypes of human tragedy.

The second chapter suggests that there is a kind of "pattern" which runs through the succession of individual tragedies which O'Neill wrote. This pattern was biographical in origin, but it has always lain implicit in all his dramas. It was suggested in an article published in his lifetime, and it was affirmed by him in a personal letter. The pattern is general, of course, and it may be described from many different approaches in many different terms —philosophical, psychological, dramatic, literary. Different writers have already suggested different aspects of it. But the very fact of its existence contributes to the fascination of "O'Neill."

The central chapters of this book (Chapter Three through Seven) describe and criticize O'Neill's best plays individually. The descriptions and critiques are as concrete and detailed as possible because the earlier generalizations need concrete realization and illustration. But such a detailed analysis of all the forty-eight plays which O'Neill published or produced would be impossible in a book of this scope. Moreover, many of his poorer plays were specifically disowned by the author, and they have also been mercifully forgotten by all but specialists. This book arbitrarily selects his twenty best plays, and (except for occasional references in Chapter One) omits the rest. The full complement of his plays is listed in the Bibliography, but the twenty plays discussed are listed in the Chronology.

This limitation to O'Neill's "best" plays has, of course, limited the negative criticism also. And the focus of attention on the larger biographical and thematic aspects of his plays has limited technical and stylistic criticism. But the most important negative criticism of O'Neill has always been directed, precisely, at his "best" plays. And his chief critics have always attacked his general philosophy of life and of tragedy, as well as his larger treatment of these dramatic themes. The concluding chapter of this book discusses the chief criticisms of his work. And in order to clarify and to answer them, it attempts to outline his theory of tragedy. For O'Neill was not only a man and a playwright— "O'Neill" was also a tragic attitude toward life.

FREDERIC I. CARPENTER

December, 1963
Berkeley, California

Acknowledgments

I am grateful to Carlotta Monterey O'Neill for permission to quote from two personal letters of Eugene O'Neill.

I am also grateful to the following publishers for permission to quote from the works to which they hold copyright (for details of publication, see "Bibliography"):

To Random House, Inc., for *The Plays of Eugene O'Neill,* collected in three volumes, 1951; and *A Moon for the Misbe-gotten,* by Eugene O'Neill. Also for *Eugene O'Neill: A Critical Study,* by Sophus K. Winther.

To Yale University Press, for *Long Day's Journey Into Night,* and *A Touch of the Poet,* by Eugene O'Neill.

To Harper and Row, Inc., for *O'Neill,* by Arthur and Barbara Gelb.

To Harcourt Brace and World, for *The Tempering of Eugene O'Neill,* by Doris Alexander.

To Dover Publications, Inc., for *Eugene O'Neill,* by Barrett H. Clark.

To Harvard University Press, for *The Haunted Heroes of Eugene O'Neill,* by Edwin A. Engel.

To Rutgers University Press, for *Eugene O'Neill and the Tragic Tension,* by Doris V. Falk.

I am grateful to the publishers and editors of periodicals, in which articles by or about O'Neill have appeared, for permission to quote. These are listed in detail in "Notes and References."

I am grateful to the publishers and editors of *College English* for permission to use parts of my essay, "The Romantic Tragedy of Eugene O'Neill," (February, 1945).

I am grateful to Travis M. Bogard and to Warren French for helpful advice in the preparation of the manuscript of this book.

Chronology

1888   Eugene Gladstone O'Neill born October 16 in New York City.

1895-   To Mount Saint Vincent, Catholic boarding school.
1900

1902-   To Betts Academy, Stamford, Connecticut.
1906

1906-   To Princeton University.
1907

1909   Married Kathleen Jenkins. "Prospecting" in Honduras.

1910   Son, Eugene Gladstone O'Neill, Jr., born. Sailed for Buenos Aires.

1911   Sailor and beachcomber.

1912   Divorced from Kathleen Jenkins. Reporter on New London *Telegraph*. To "Gaylord Farm," tuberculosis sanitarium, December 24, for six months.

1913   Copyrighted first plays: *A Wife for a Life*, and *The Web*.

1914   To Baker's Dramatic Workshop, Harvard. Published first book: *Thirst, and Other One-Act Plays*.

1916   To Provincetown. First plays produced there: *Bound East for Cardiff* and *Thirst*. November: *Bound East for Cardiff* produced in New York.

1917   *The Long Voyage Home*, and other plays, produced.

1918   Married Agnes Boulton.

1919   Son, Shane O'Neill, born.

1920   First full-length play, *Beyond the Horizon*, produced in New York, February; won Pulitzer Prize. Father, James O'Neill, died in August. *The Emperor Jones*, November.

1921   *Anna Christie*, second Pulitzer Prize play.

1922   Mother, Ellen Quinlan O'Neill, died. *The Hairy Ape*.

1923   Brother, James O'Neill, Jr., died.

1924   *All God's Chillun Got Wings. Desire Under the Elms.*

1925   Oona O'Neill born. *The Fountain.*

1926   *The Great God Brown.*

1927   *Marco Millions* published, April. *Lazarus Laughed,* November.

1928   *Strange Interlude,* third Pulitzer Prize play. Traveled in the Orient.

1929   *Dynamo.* Divorced from Agnes Boulton. Married Carlotta Monterey in France. Lived at Le Plessis.

1931   *Mourning Becomes Electra.*

1932   Built "Casa Genotta," Sea Island, Georgia.

1933   *Ah, Wilderness!*

1934   *Days Without End.*

1936   Won Nobel Prize for Literature. Ill health.

1937   Built "Tao House," Danville, California.

1939   Wrote *The Iceman Cometh.*

1940   Began writing *Long Day's Journey Into Night.*

1943   Finished writing *A Moon for the Misbegotten.*

1945   Returned to New York.

1946   *The Iceman Cometh* produced.

1950   Eugene O'Neill, Jr., died.

1953   Eugene Gladstone O'Neill died, November 27, Boston.

1956   *The Iceman Cometh* revived: record run of 565 performances. *Long Day's Journey Into Night* produced; fourth Pulitzer Prize play.

1957   *A Touch of the Poet.*

Eugene O'Neill

CHAPTER 1

O'Neill: Tragic Agonist

O N December 13, 1953, two weeks after Eugene O'Neill's death, New York *Times* critic Brooks Atkinson mourned: "A giant writer has dropped off the earth; a great spirit and our greatest dramatist have left us, and our theatre world is now a smaller, more ordinary place." Other critics had already expressed appreciation of the man and of his work, and many had used the word "great." But few had suggested so poignantly the sense of personal loss and the feeling that the spirit of the man was, somehow, greater than his work. By universal consent O'Neill had become "our greatest dramatist," with his plays already preserved in the anthologies, and his career already chronicled in the literary histories. But the brooding spirit of the man, glimpsed in his lifetime through his dark, dreaming, yet strangely vivid and compelling eyes, seemed in danger of being forgotten.

In 1953 "a great spirit" had left us, and might soon have been forgotten, along with the funeral oratory and the encomiums, except that the man had already composed the dramatic autobiography of the spirit in *Long Day's Journey Into Night.* Three years after his death this play was first published and produced. From beyond the grave, as it were, O'Neill returned to act out his own life's personal tragedy. And in the same year his semi-autobiographical *The Iceman Cometh,* which was successfully revived on the New York stage, seemed to reinforce the impression that all of his drama had been autobiographical. *A Moon for the Misbegotten* had earlier told of the tragic life of his brother, Jamie, with whose fate he had been so deeply involved. And so the dead playwright gradually assumed a new role in man's minds, one very different from that of "our greatest

dramatist" or of "a great spirit"—the role of the tormented
agonist in the tragic drama of his own life.

It had long been known that the young O'Neill had sown
his wild oats, and had experienced many colorful adventures
at sea and in foreign lands. In 1919, even before his first full-
length play had been published or produced, he had furnished
a biographical sketch to Barrett Clark, which was published in
successive editions of *Eugene O'Neill: The Man and His Plays.*
O'Neill's life before the mast had obviously furnished the background for his first successful plays of the sea, and his six
months in a tuberculosis sanitarium had contributed to his drama
The Straw. He had cheerfully admitted to monumental drinking
bouts in his youth, and he had even described his attempt at
suicide as a kind of riotous farce. But, with the publication of his
final autobiographical tragedies, these youthful adventures and
escapades took on a new, darker meaning.

As the motives behind his escapes to the sea, his drinking
bouts, and his desperate attempt at suicide became clear, the
romantic aura of adventure and the comic overtones were
dispelled. The physical and nervous breakdown which had led
him to the tuberculosis sanitarium became the archetype of all
confusion and tragedy. And what had earlier seemed the
objective facts of the biographical sketch of a promising
dramatist now came to seem the subjective material of tragedy
itself. The playwright became the tragic agonist, and his life a
drama more violently theatrical than that of any of his fictional
heroes.

The remarkable success of *Long Day's Journey* produced a
strange effect upon the popular imagination. Although the play
itself had described O'Neill's tragedy in full, realistic detail, it
appealed so vividly to men's minds that other authors felt
themselves impelled to improve upon and to elaborate it. In
1959 Max Wylie published a lurid novel entitled *Trouble in the
Flesh*, whose hero was "Seton Farrier, the greatest dramatist of
his time," but whose family life followed closely the known facts
of O'Neill's. In the same year Crosswell Bowen published a
somewhat journalistic, overwritten biography entitled *The Curse
of the Misbegotten: A Tale of the House of O'Neill.* That some
mysterious kind of curse rested upon O'Neill and his family
seemed obvious; but why his father, whose life had been almost

perfectly successful, married to a woman whom he had treated with almost perfect consideration, could have sired children and grandchildren somehow "misbegotten" remained unexplained. What was this mysterious "trouble"—this tragic "curse"?

The mystery and the apparent inexplicability of the known facts of O'Neill's life have continued to inspire biographers and critics, and neither the end nor the explanation is in sight. In 1962 two good biographies, one by Doris Alexander and the other by Arthur and Barbara Gelb, were published; and both narrated many important facts previously unknown, and suggested valuable new interpretations. Meanwhile more than a dozen authors have announced that they are working on new biographies or critical interpretations of the man and his work. The challenge of "the unknown"—that same "mystery and spell" which had lured O'Neill in his own lifetime—continues to invest the character of the playwright himself.

The facts of the life are mostly known and are easily available in the biographies. But the problems and the interpretations which these facts suggest, and the challenge which they offer to biographers and readers alike, are only beginning to become clear. Therefore this chapter will focus upon these problems and interpretations, and it will narrate the biographical facts necessary for the illustration of these.

I   *The Start of the Journey*

When *Long Day's Journey* was first published, many people assumed that it was pure autobiography and accepted its actions at face value. The closeness of the story to the known facts of O'Neill's life, and the apparently simple realism of its presentation easily convinced the unwary that this tragic drama was "the truth." Gradually, of course, it became apparent that it was not the whole truth—O'Neill's first marriage, which had already ended in divorce at the time of the drama's action, was not mentioned. And even more gradually it became apparent that this "autobiography," even when it told the truth as its chief protagonist may have seen it, distorted some of the facts, just as it obviously ignored others. By the very perfection of its artistic verisimilitude it emphasized the problem of the relationship of biographic fact to artistic fiction. How is life transmuted into art by the alembic of the imagination?

The central problem upon which the interpretation of *Long Day's Journey* turns is that of the character and relationship of James and Mary Tyrone, who closely correspond to the actual James and Ellen (or Ella) O'Neill, Eugene's father and mother. The play develops their characters and relationship dramatically, and realistically.

Like the actual James O'Neill, James Tyrone is the son of an Irish immigrant who deserted his wife when the boy was ten to return to Ireland. Like James O'Neill, James Tyrone was forced to work continuously as a boy. This childhood experience bred in him an exaggerated consciousness of the importance of money, which (in the play) is the root of all evil. And James Tyrone, like James O'Neill, continued to work hard, became a successful actor, and soon rose to the top of his profession. As he tells his son (with exact names and dates taken from James O'Neill's actual career), he acted Shakespeare with Edwin Booth, who testified: "That young man is playing Othello better than I ever did!" But then Tyrone says: "I married your mother," and needed even more money. Soon after this he achieved such great financial success as the hero of a romantic melodrama (exactly as James O'Neill did in *Monte Cristo*), that he gave up serious acting and spent the rest of his professional career making money ("from thirty-five to forty thousand net profit a season!"). Thus James Tyrone prostituted his artistic career to money-making, and lost his own self-respect. The tragedy of *Long Day's Journey*, therefore, is motivated in part by James Tyrone's miserliness and materialism. And these biographical facts almost exactly correspond to those of Eugene's father, James O'Neill.

But James Tyrone's miserliness is exaggerated far beyond the actual facts of James O'Neill's actual life. The fictional Tyrone is accused of two cardinal sins in his relationship with his wife. Most important, he is said to have hired a "cheap quack" of a doctor to care for her when their youngest son, Edmund (the actual Eugene), was born. And this fictional quack is said to have prescribed the morphine which started the mother's tragic addiction to dope. And even before this, Tyrone is said to have forced his wife to live in a cheap house in New London, which so humiliated her that she could never feel it was "a home": "I'd never felt it was my home. It was wrong from the start. Everything was done the cheapest way."

But these two fictional acts of Tyrone's life were so exaggerated that they seem almost the opposite of the actual truth. Although the actual James O'Neill was often miserly by habit, he loved and idolized his wife so greatly that he often spent more on her than he could afford. It was precisely in order to support his wife in the manner to which she had become accustomed (her father had been a successful businessman), that James O'Neill prostituted his artistic career to achieve spectacular financial success. Truth is often stranger, and more complex, than fiction.

In fact James O'Neill had always been extremely sensitive to the problems of his young bride, who, as the wife of a traveling actor, could seldom live long in any one place. This sensitiveness had been intensified when their second son had died in infancy (just as did the second son of the fictional Tyrones) while the parents were absent together "on the road." Therefore, in order to provide his wife a permanent "home," James O'Neill had built an expensive house for Ellen "of the finest materials. . . . The Boston *Times* reported that the house had cost $40,000—a fortune in 1883."[1] Moreover, he had built it in New London, where many of his wife's relatives lived. If Ellen O'Neill could never feel that this was "home," the fault was not his.

The truth of the charge that the father's miserliness in hiring "cheap quacks" had caused the mother's addiction to morphine is more uncertain. After eighty years it is impossible to determine just what caused it, but two facts are clear. At that time even the best doctors were not fully aware of the habit-forming dangers of the drug. And, either just before, or years after Eugene's actual birth (biographers do not agree), his mother was operated on for cancer of the breast: James O'Neill took her to the most famous specialists in Europe, where the operation was successfully performed.[2] Ellen O'Neill had been sick near the time of Eugene's birth, and she suffered from dope addiction years after; but it is doubtful that either his father's miserliness or his own birth was the actual cause. Probably Eugene himself never knew the true facts of his mother's tragedy and of his own "misbegetting." And surely his autobiographical drama describes the psychological truth as he believed it. But dramatic fiction and biographical fact remain far apart.

The facts of O'Neill's actual biography and the fictions of *Long Day's Journey* approach one another somewhat more closely in the relationship of the young Eugene (named Edmund in the play) and his father. Again, miserliness is the issue, and in the play James Tyrone is described as planning, in order to save money, to send his sick son to "a state farm" for the treatment of his tuberculosis. Actually, Eugene spent six months in an excellent private sanitarium, "Gaylord Farm," where his tuberculosis was cured. But it is also true that Eugene was actually sent to the "Fairfield County State Tuberculosis Sanitarium" for two days before being transferred to this private sanitarium.[3] The confused reasons are not known, but the relationship of James O'Neill with his son Eugene was—both in fact and in fiction—ambivalent.

Again, the truth was more complicated than the fiction. Although James O'Neill, like James Tyrone, was often miserly, he only shared the common experiences and attitudes of his generation, and of the American immigrant past. In 1912 thrift was a cardinal American virtue, but a generation later thrift sometimes seemed like miserliness. And even more important, James O'Neill, in his relationship with Eugene, faced the difficult problem of bringing up the "poor little rich boy." His older son Jamie had, indeed, become completely spoiled. And throughout Eugene's youth the father sought to limit the son's spending money and to discipline his wasteful habits in order to teach him the value of hard work. But the young Eugene, in his turn, saw only that his father had lots of money and that there was no need for him to work. Theirs was the universal conflict of two generations and of the different *mores* appropriate to each.

Beyond this conflict, however, loomed that of the artist with the philistine—a conflict limited to no one time or country. James O'Neill believed that his sons should work for their living; and in Jamie's case he was right—his failure lay in not enforcing his belief. But Eugene, the future artist, was to work for a living with his imagination and, therefore, the future artist felt outraged at his father's insistence that he should work physically to earn money. But his father believed in hard work and in success. Only after Eugene became successful and won the

Pulitzer Prize shortly before his father's death did the two become happily reconciled. Since this final reconciliation between father and son provides the dramatic resolution of the tragedy of *Long Day's Journey*, it is true to the spirit—but not to the letter—of biographical fact.

The fictional mother of *Long Day's Journey*, Mary Tyrone, is probably closer to actuality than is any other character. Ellen Quinlan O'Neill had been brought up in the genteel, Victorian tradition of the late nineteenth century. A convent-reared girl, she was beautiful, innocent, romantic, and utterly unworldly. In fact, she was the exact opposite of her future husband, who had been bred in the school of hard knocks, was experienced, practical, successful, and very sophisticated. Ellen Quinlan's extreme idealization, both of her future husband and of life in general, partly inspired both the artistic tragedy of Eugene O'Neill and the actual tragedies of her own life and of her sons.

When Ellen Quinlan married James O'Neill, she expected the impossible, and—in so far as her husband was able to provide it by conscious effort—she got it. At the time of her marriage (to a man eleven years her senior), she knew that her future husband had lived with an actress and that there was talk of an illegitimate son; that he belonged utterly to the world of the theater, of whose morals most respectable people (including her mother) disapproved; and that his profession inevitably required constant traveling and homelessness. But the fictional "Count of Monte Cristo" was able to escape from his dungeon and to conquer the world every matinee and evening, and James O'Neill *was* "the Count of Monte Cristo."

After their marriage James always did his best to protect his wife from the roughness of the theater (he forbade swearing and loose talk in her presence); he shielded her as best he could from the scandal of a paternity suit (once he had grown rich, he was a fair target); he remained perfectly faithful to his marriage vows throughout his life (Mary Tyrone remembers: "In all those thirty-six years, there has never been a breath of scandal about him. I mean with any other woman"); he provided generously for her comfort and security, in so far as money could provide; he tried to build her a "home"; and he even gave up the theater during several periods to care for her.

But he could not escape from his own past, he could not

change the conditions of his chosen profession, and he could not prevent those tragedies common to all men—such as the death of his second son. Finally, he could not wholly change himself. Although he loved only his wife among all women, he continued to love sociability and the whisky that went with it: sometimes he drank too much, and failed to come home for dinner. But by all ordinary standards, the marriage of James and Ellen O'Neill was successful, and should not have resulted in tragedy—either in actuality or in fiction. Why, then, the tragedy?

II *An American Tragedy*

"None of us can help the things life has done to us. They're done before you realize it, and once they're done they make you do other things until at last everything comes between you and what you'd like to be, and you've lost your true self forever." This speech by Mary Tyrone describes in colloquial terms the philosophy which O'Neill affirmed all his life and which he particularly embodied in *Long Day's Journey.* Although the four characters of the autobiographical drama seem to wound and to destroy one another by their constant bickerings and conflicts, their true tragedy is caused, rather, by what "life" has done to them—by the unseen forces of their heredity and environment. And these unseen forces may also be said to have caused the actual tragedy of Eugene O'Neill. Not his flamboyant and sometimes parsimonious father, nor his gentle and defeated mother, nor his rebellious and profligate brother caused his tragic agony. The cause lay, rather, in their common heritage as Irish Catholic immigrants to an alien land, and in the conditions of life which the father's theatrical profession imposed upon them all.

"My poor mother washed and scrubbed for the Yanks by the day," James Tyrone remembers. And the feeling of social inferiority which this experience recalled, as well as the feeling of national antagonism suggested by the phrase "the Yanks," echoes through all of O'Neill's life and plays. Meanwhile, the two Tyrone brothers sneeringly call their father "The Beautiful Voice." And although the mother pretends to defend him, she constantly harps upon the homelessness which his profession has forced upon them. Because Eugene was born the son of an

Irish immigrant and because he was brought up in the homeless world of the theater, his life seemed destined for tragedy.

Curiously Eugene's identification with his Irish ancestry grew stronger, rather than weaker, over the years. The first character to speak in the first of his "S. S. Glencairn" plays was "Driscoll," who exclaimed "irritably": "Will ye listen to them naygurs?" The young O'Neill sympathized with all the sailors of the ship, but this early Irishman scorned "them naygurs" as his author would never do. Later, O'Neill sympathized more completely with "the hairy ape," who could never "belong" to American society and who embodied the psychology of the eternal outsider—of Irishman and Negro alike. But his identification with his Irish ancestry became total in his final play when Josie Hogan, with "the map of Ireland stamped upon her face," pronounced a final benediction on brother "James Tyrone, Jr.": "May you rest forever in forgiveness and peace."

But his father, James O'Neill, had done his best to escape his Irish heritage. In order to achieve success as an actor, he had consciously suppressed his Irish brogue. Ridiculed for his country manners and his Irish accent, he had tried to make himself over into an American gentleman. And he had become universally loved and admired in the world of the theater to which he "belonged." Nevertheless, as *Long Day's Journey* suggests, he and his wife had never been fully accepted by the class-conscious society of New London. And the sensitive young playwright became acutely conscious of this rejection.

The experience of Irishness common to all the O'Neills and the feeling of alienation that went with it were typical of twentieth-century America—but comparatively rare in the earlier America of Emerson and Whitman's time. By 1900 the "Yankee" society of New England had crystallized into a self-conscious, middle-class culture to which the later immigrants felt themselves alien. Their social inferiority and their cultural alienation have been described by modern novelists such as Dreiser and James T. Farrell, as well as by O'Neill. Indeed, much of the tragic spirit of modern American literature, with its emphatic rejection of the earlier optimism, may have sprung from this feeling of cultural alienation. In 1800, all Americans were immigrants from an old England to a new England. But in 1900 the new immigrants to an established America came from alien lands and spoke with foreign accents. O'Neill chronicled the tragedies of Chris and Anna Christopherson, of Brutus "the Emperor" Jones, and of Jim "Crow" Harris, as well as those of James and Edmund Tyrone.

But these Irish who came to America around the turn of the century were no ordinary immigrants. For Irishmen had long been aliens and outsiders even in their own ancestral home in the "British" Isles. They had always opposed the authority and the society of their English overlords. As John Henry Raleigh has phrased it, they had suffered from a "Judas complex."[4] Just as James and Eugene O'Neill sought to overcome the hostile and philistine society of the new world by means of histrionic art and dramatic imagination, so the Irish had always sought to overcome their English conquerors. It is no accident that Eugene O'Neill's dramas have been most highly praised by Irishmen, such as Synge and Yeats,[5] but have been most violently attacked by conservative British critics.

Added to Eugene's heritage as the son of an Irish immigrant was his heritage of the theater. Indeed, the two were often the same, since the Irish have excelled at acting. (There are curious parallels between the story of Synge's *Playboy of the Western World* and O'Neill's own story.) And this heritage of the theater helps to explain, psychologically, the mingling of actual autobiography with fictional tragedy throughout O'Neill's life. To the Irish immigrant's uncertainty as to his nationality was added the actor's uncertainty as to his true identity. James O'Neill became, in a sense, the Count of Monte Cristo; and his sons called him the Beautiful Voice. In identifying himself with his actor's role, had James O'Neill "lost his true self forever"? And what, exactly, was the "true self" of an Irish immigrant actor—or of his son? Eugene would spend his lifetime seeking.

Beyond the psychological effect of his theatrical heritage, the practical effect of his father's way of life loomed even greater. The homelessness of which Mary Tyrone complained in 1912 had been caused not by James's parsimony but by the practical necessities of an actor's life. And this homelessness "caused" the tragedy of the son as well as the tragedy of the mother.

Eugene O'Neill was born in a hotel in New York City where his father was acting. In Eugene's early years he never knew a stable "home." At the early age of seven he was sent away

to Mount Saint Vincent, a Catholic boarding school. And throughout childhood he seldom lived any length of time with his parents.
His most vivid, painful memory in later years was of his
loneliness at boarding schools. And particularly he recalled being
forced to spend Christmas vacation at his first school because
his parents were away "on the road." To his third wife he confessed forty years later the agony caused by this "betrayal" by
his parents at a time when all the other children had gone home
to celebrate Christmas with their parents.[6] The first and deepest
unhappiness of his life was that of homelessness—both psychological and physical.

But beyond the physical and the psychological homelessness
caused by his Irish immigrant ancestry and his theatrical
heritage, a deeper feeling of spiritual rootlessness resulted from
his early experiences with Catholicism. The Catholic boarding
school to which the young boy was sent inevitably became
associated with his feelings of "betrayal" by his parents. And this
natural association was not dispelled (as ideally it might have
been) by the administration of the school. For Mount Saint
Vincent emphasized formal discipline and regulation rather than
the home-like warmth which the lonely child needed. In later
years he recalled chiefly the black robes and the white starched
collars of the nuns. And he progressively associated their lack
of emotional warmth with the Catholic religion. After five years
at this boarding school and after two more at a Catholic day
school, he finally rebelled against his Catholic heritage. At
fourteen he was sent away to Betts Academy—a non-sectarian
preparatory school in Connecticut.

Thus the one element of his heritage which might have
provided him with a spiritual "home" failed him. Throughout
his life he was to wrestle with the problem of religious faith,
and once, in *Days Without End*, he seemed to be returning to
the church. But from earliest childhood his life had been set
in the pattern of homelessness by his parents, and Catholicism
never provided a foster home. The final dramas of his later
years describe his confrontation and acceptance of this tragic lot.

And yet the very elements of his heritage which most caused
his personal tragedy, and set him most apart from the American
society about him, paradoxically made his tragedy most American.
For the typically "American" experience—as contrasted with the

typical experience of the old world—has always been characterized by insecurity and homelessness, isolation, and often
alienation.[7] The Irish immigration which introduced the O'Neills
to an alien land, the migratory profession which necessitated
his family's homelessness, and his own consequent alienation
from the religious faith which had sustained his parents—all were
typically American. His own tragic agony and the imaginative
dramas which he produced merely realized and greatly intensified the elements of tragedy inherent in the American experience
from the beginning.

III   "Trouble in the Flesh"

One afternoon when the young Eugene returned early from
school, he surprised his mother in the act of giving herself a
"hypo" of morphine. At first unaware of the meaning of what
he had seen, the later realization of it shocked him profoundly.
And his mother's addiction was certainly the precipitating fact
of his own tragic emotional turmoil, as it was of Edmund Tyrone's
in *Long Day's Journey*. Moreover, this fact was physical and
tangible. A novel entitled *Trouble in the Flesh* embroidered
fictionally on the life of "our greatest dramatist," and it exaggerated this physical fact to suggest that the hero had perhaps
been poisoned by his mother's dope addiction before his own
birth: that his tragedy, therefore, was physically determined.
The same assumption of some physical cause of tragedy is
implied by the early biographer's title: *The Curse of the Misbegotten*. Certainly some physical flaw in his "begetting" would
more easily and simply explain his tragedy. And certainly the
"trouble" which he somehow inherited did find physical expression in his own "flesh." But, just as the dramatic tragedies which
he imagined all turned on psychological causes, so probably did
his own life's tragedy.

Traditionally youth is beset by the troubles of the flesh, and
O'Neill's certainly was. And traditionally the morals of the
theater have been free, as his were. A generation earlier his
father had lived with actresses and had also begotten an
illegitimate son before his own marriage, so why should his son
be different? For Eugene belonged to the world of the theater
also. Even after having been sent away to boarding school, he

often went to New York for weekends; there his brother Jamie helped guide him through the world of parties and chorus girls. Meanwhile at the academy his classmates were acutely conscious of his sophistication and of the difference between his world and theirs. And so, when he went on to Princeton, he had already graduated from the school of worldly experience.

The free and easy morals of the theater came naturally to Eugene. But what made him different from his father was his consciousness of belonging also to another world. For after his marriage his father had tried to make himself over into the image of a model family man and solid citizen. And Eugene and his brother joined in rebelling against this acquired image of social propriety. Therefore their trouble in the flesh was seldom simple and natural (as the father's had been); instead, it was rebellious and violent. James, Jr., for instance, was finally expelled from Notre Dame for squiring a famous prostitute to a formal college dance on a wager—and the act of bravado is typical. The young Eugene repeatedly indulged in similar escapades in order to taunt his father and to shock his respectable classmates.

But Eugene also loved his mother, and he clung to her image of purity, which Mary Tyrone so vividly embodies in *Long Day's Journey.* Separated from the world of chorus girls, there were also "nice" girls. And as he went through Betts Academy and Princeton and explored the cosmopolitan world of New York, he also met some of these. On a double date arranged by a friend, he became attracted to a nice girl named Kathleen Jenkins, and later he saw her often. When he learned that she had become pregnant, he faced the age-old dilemma. His friend who had introduced them insisted that he should marry her, but his father (remembering his own youthful troubles) advised against it. Eugene "solved" the dilemma by marrying and then immediately deserting her. Wholly confused, he wished only to forget the whole incident. Thirty years later, he omitted this episode from the autobiographical log of his *Long Day's Journey Into Night*.

Meanwhile the problem of liquor accompanied the problem of women, as it traditionally has. Like his Irish ancestors, James O'Neill loved his whisky, and a bottle of it was always available in *Long Day's Journey.* James sometimes drank too much, and one evening on his way home from town he fell off a railroad trestle and almost killed himself. But his drinking always remained social. His son Jamie, however, became a hopeless alcoholic and died in a sanitarium at the age of forty-five. Meanwhile, Eugene faced the problem of alcoholism all his life, and eventually overcame it. But it was a long, doubtful struggle.

Eugene's most famous drunken escapade was probably his least important: he is fabled to have been expelled from Princeton for throwing a beer bottle through President Woodrow Wilson's window. Actually he was only temporarily suspended (along with two friends) for throwing stones and for other minor acts of vandalism on the way home from a drunken evening in town. Moreover, the incident merely marked the climax of a series of such events—he was trying probably to get himself expelled, for he felt more at home in New York City. Even where drinking was recognized as a gentleman's pastime, he drank in excess.

After his first marriage and just before his twenty-first birthday, he sailed away on what he later dignified as a "prospecting expedition" to Honduras. Actually he went with a friend of his father, and the journey was more of an escape from past troubles than a search for new opportunities. But it introduced him to foreign lands, and it gave him firsthand experience of the actual jungle. And even though engineered by his father and guided by others, the trip started him on three years of wandering and adventure which widened his horizon beyond that of his own country, made him aware of a "primitive" way of life unlike that of his own people, and showed him that human suffering was caused not only by human institutions but also by nature itself. After a few months he was invalided home with jungle fever and arrived in New York where his father tried to get him to work in the theater. But again he ran away—this time on his own initiative.

In the spring of 1910 he signed on a sailing ship for Buenos Aires—the *Charles Racine*. And during the two-month voyage South he fell in love with the sea and the life of the sailor. Like Melville and Jack London before him, he not only found escape from the confusions of the past, but he enjoyed new experiences which were to inspire his future writing. Returning to New York on the *Ikalis* a year later, he had learned to know firsthand all the colorful crew who were to people the S. S. *Glencairn*; and he had experienced subjectively the exaltation of "the beauty and singing rhythm" of the sea, which he was to celebrate in *Long Day's Journey.*

But meanwhile he had spent many months on the beach at Buenos Aires. During this time he "worked" unsuccessfully at a series of jobs—with Westinghouse, with Swift Packing Company, and with Singer Sewing Machine Company—but most of his time he spent drinking with a variety of friends and acquaintances of the waterfront. Many years later he inscribed a volume of his plays for an Argentine library, expressing the "doubt that there was a single park bench in Buenos Aires that had not served him as a bed."[8] And when he returned to New York in 1911, the same pattern of life continued. He made no effort to see either his father and mother, or the wife who had recently born his first son, Eugene Gladstone O'Neill, Jr. Instead, he took a room above "Jimmy-the-Priest's" saloon (described in the first scene of *Anna Christie*), and he drank steadily with sailors and friends (many of whom later appeared in Harry Hope's saloon in *The Iceman Cometh*).

For O'Neill as for Melville, the sea and the life of a sailor became symbols both of liberation and exaltation, and of frustration and continuing despair. And the next voyage for which he signed combined both. On a passenger liner plying to Europe and back, he experienced the mechanization of the modern ship, and the social snobbishness which he dramatized (in exaggerated form) in *The Hairy Ape*. When he finally returned to New York in October, 1911, his life on the sea had ended. And "the iceman" was at hand.

The next twelve months of his life were crucial. There seemed no place to go but down. Although he usually lived above the saloon on the waterfront, he returned to his father for financial assistance. During this time, in order to help his wife get a divorce (according to the laws of New York State, the only grounds for divorce were adultery), he arranged to be caught *in flagrante delicto* with a prostitute. He continued to drink even more heavily at Jimmy-the-Priest's, and one day he learned that one of his favorite sailors, Driscoll, had just committed suicide by jumping overboard in mid-ocean. Soon after this, an old theatrical friend and roommate, Jimmy Byth, committed suicide by jumping from a bedroom window (much like Don Parritt in *The Iceman*). And soon afterwards, Eugene himself attempted suicide by swallowing an overdose of veronal tablets. He was taken to a hospital and revived. But although he later described the suicide attempt as a farce, and later still wrote a one-act play, *Exorcism,* which dramatized the incident as a means by which the hero "exorcised" his past sins, it was not very funny at the time.

After all this, his father took him away to New London for the summer and fall of 1912, where the events described in *Long Day's Journey* took place. Recovering somewhat from his alcoholism and his despair, he got a job as roving reporter for a local newspaper, which he enjoyed. At this time he also enjoyed some family outings and neighborhood friendships of the kind described years later in *Ah, Wilderness!* But the physical and emotional effects of his recent life had undermined his health; at the end of the year he was invalided to a tuberculosis sanitarium.

During the first six months of 1913 at the sanitarium, he began to write his first plays. And having suddenly found a vocation and a reason for living, he attempted to make himself over in the image of a new ideal. But, like his father before him, he never succeeded in re-forming himself. In the years of success to come, the old black moods sometimes returned, and he escaped to some "Jimmy-the-Priest's" or "Hell Hole," until some friend found him and brought him "home." Trouble always remained.

IV   *"Light on the Path"*

The transformation of young Eugene from playboy and beachcomber to dedicated playwright was not so sudden as it has sometimes seemed. The six months of enforced quiet at the sanitarium during which he faced down the problems of his life did mark a dramatic break with his past. But even during his playboy years he had been unconsciously preparing for his future profession. His bookish education—especially the informal aspects of it—had helped. And the vague philosophy of life which he developed from it was more positive than it seemed.

When Eugene was eighteen, he first read Nietzsche's *Thus Spake Zarathustra.* Decades later he declared that *"Zarathustra* has influenced me more than any book I've ever read." The poetic exhortations of this imaginary prophet, combined with the more sober philosophy of Nietzsche's *The Birth of Tragedy*, not only inspired the young playwright but suggested his future theory of tragedy. When Zarathustra proclaimed: "You must have chaos in you to give birth to a dancing star. I tell you that you still have chaos in you," he spoke to the young man's present condition in terms of future prophecy. And when Nietzsche traced the birth of Greek tragedy to the pagan rites of the god Dionysus, he seemed to combine history with prophecy. For the young playwright was indeed a worshiper of Dionysus, and he felt chaos within himself. But he also felt within himself the potential "birth of a dancing star," and he dreamed of the drunken laughter of Dionysus transformed into the liberated laughter of Lazarus. To O'Neill, Nietzsche suggested the element of transcendence implicit in all tragedy.

This transcendental philosophy which Nietzsche prophesied was, of course, tragic; and sometimes it seemed wholly pessimistic. The similar passages of poetry and philosophy which the autobiographical Edmund Tyrone declaimed to his father in *Long Day's Journey* were even more emphatically pessimistic, and they were therefore branded "morbid" by the father. Yet the element of transcendence in them is more significant than their pessimism. And Eugene himself may have been prepared to welcome Nietzsche by reading the volumes of Emerson in his father's library,[9] for the German philosopher himself had been inspired by the American. Or he may have found some of this transcendental mysticism in the Irish poets and playwrights that he read both then and later. But ultimately this mysticism derived from an Oriental philosophy which had influenced both Emerson and Nietzsche, and—later—Yeats and Synge. "The mystery and spell of the East which lures me in the books I've read," may have been vague, but it was fundamental.

Just as Nietzsche's *Zarathustra* influenced Eugene more than any other book he ever read, so Terry Carlin influenced him more than any other friend. Like Nietzsche, a worshiper of Dionysus, Terry Carlin had met O'Neill about 1915 in the "Hell Hole." A fellow Irishman (born Terence O'Carolan), Terry possessed a love of mystical philosophy combined with a gift for words with which he enthralled the literate and the illiterate alike. He had been mentor to a young Hindu mystic named Dhan Gopal Mukerji, and now he preached a philosophy combining Nietzsche with the wisdom of the East. Most important, he introduced Eugene to a book of mystical theosophy entitled *Light on the Path*, which combined Oriental wisdom with Occidental psychology.

Neither Terry Carlin nor *Light on the Path* was philosophically "respectable," but both served to introduce the young playwright to the wisdom of the East and to develop the transcendental philosophy of tragedy which Nietzsche had first described. When Terry and Eugene settled in Provincetown in the summer of 1916, they inscribed above the door of their room a quotation from *Light on the Path*: "Before the eyes can see they must be incapable of tears. . . . Before the soul can stand . . . its feet must be washed in the blood of the heart." And they often read aloud its passages of mixed Oriental-Western religion and psychology: "Seek the life beyond individuality. . . . Seek it by plunging into the mysterious depths of your own being. . . . For within you is the light of the world, the only light that can be shed on the Path."[10]

This "philosophy" was not formal, and certainly its mysticism was vague; but it helped O'Neill to formulate a theory of tragedy which was to become both distinctive and modern. This theory of tragedy may perhaps, be summarized in a sentence. Through tragedy salvation may be achieved. Or, as Jean Paul Sartre was later to express the idea, "Life begins on the far side of despair."

Meanwhile Eugene was steeping himself in the works of the great dramatists, both ancient and modern. His father, of course, had supervised his education in Shakespeare, and he once memorized all of *Macbeth* to win a wager from "the old man." Similarly he read widely in classical Greek drama. But he also witnessed the theatrical production of many famous plays, ancient and modern, for his father could usually supply free tickets. When the Irish "Abbey Players" came to New York in 1911, he became an enthusiastic attendant. He knew and admired Ibsen, both as reader and as theater-goer. But most of all he valued August Strindberg, who, because he was less widely known and admired, became more of a personal discovery. Many years later and after winning the Nobel Prize, O'Neill took the occasion to emphasize his continuing debt to the

Swedish dramatist: "For me he remains, as Nietzsche remains, in his sphere, the master, still to this day more modern than any of us, still our leader."

The best known (but probably the least important) aspect of his preparation for his future career was his participation in Professor George Pierce Baker's "dramatic workshop" at Harvard. After his decision to become a playwright, his father sent him to this pioneering experiment in the education of aspiring playwrights. But, although Eugene admired Professor Baker and wrote many dramatic compositions for his course, he learned comparatively little from it. Mostly he discovered what he did *not* want to do—he did not want to follow the conventional dramatists of his time. And, when the year ended, he felt little inclination ever to return to the academic life.

And so, by a series of rejections and rebellions, he arrived at the threshold of his career. Already he had written a number of apprentice plays, and his father had financed the publication of a volume of them. He was soon to enjoy his first professional triumph at Provincetown, and after that his rise to fame was swift. But during these years he continued to live in Greenwich Village, in and above the "Hell Hole." And with Terry Carlin he continued to drink and talk with anarchists and prostitutes. And living with them, he also shared their confused ideals of free love and anarchism.

But it is important to realize that "free love" and "anarchism" were positive ideals, as well as attitudes of rebellion and negation. The free love of Greenwich Village did not include the idealization of prostitutes; rather, it imagined their redemption—as later dramatized in *Anna Christie*. And the "anarchism" of the "Hell Hole" did not include the idealization of the Communist state; it preached the ideal abolition of all states. The individual was all-important; conventional society, nothing.

These ideals, as O'Neill practiced them at this time, found vivid embodiment in his strangely mixed relationship with his two friends, John Reed and his wife Louise Bryant. Although Louise was legally married to John, she believed in free love; and she loved Eugene. When John was away making speeches or in the hospital, she lived happily and illegally with Eugene. At Provincetown the two acted together in his first plays. Later, when she and John went to Russia together to observe and to celebrate the Revolution, John experienced and wrote his famous *Ten Days that Shook the World*; and there he died, a hero of the Revolution (and a victim of his weak constitution and some typhus germs). When Louise returned to America, she learned that Eugene had married Agnes Boulton; but she still loved him and expected him to share his love with her also. But now he felt differently; with the approval of Agnes he tactfully ended the whole affair.

The tangled loves of John, Louise Reed, and Eugene illustrate vividly the naïvely confused idealisms of the time. Many years later Eugene dramatized some of these confusions in the story of *Strange Interlude*,[11] whose heroine shared her ideal love with three men. And then critics complained of the artificiality of the plot and the Freudianism of the psychology without realizing that the author had himself experienced these tragically mixed loves and idealisms. *Light on the Path* had proclaimed that "the feet of the soul must be washed in the blood of the heart." This mixed but vivid metaphor may stand for the confused but genuine idealism of O'Neill's early life.

V *Three Wives for Three Lives*

Eugene O'Neill was married three times and divorced twice; he deserted two wives, and was deserted (for a brief period) by the third; he quarreled, ran off, returned, and made up. But never for long did he enjoy peace from the furies which drove him. The stories of his escapades, which are legion, give the impression that he rushed from one emotional experience to the other without rhyme or reason. But just as his dramas describe the conflicting emotions of tragic protagonists in significant patterns—*Strange Interlude*, for instance, objectifies the conflicting loves of Nina Leeds for her "three men"—so his own emotional conflicts were objectified in his relations with his three wives. Since these conflicts persisted throughout his life, each marriage was troubled by the conflicting needs which could not be satisfied by any one relationship. But his own conflicts found expression in each of his successive marriages; and his emotional life may be described in relation to them.

That O'Neill's character was complex, and that it included at least two different "selves," was emphasized by Brooks Atkinson's obituary remark: "a great spirit and our greatest dramatist have left us." But funeral oratory traditionally speaks only good concerning the dead, and in life O'Neill was often spectacularly "bad." Besides the two admirable selves described by Atkinson, his early self had often been violent and rebellious, and this destructive self continued to cause him trouble throughout his life. Recently *Esquire* magazine published an article entitled: "Portrait of a Nobel Prize Winner as a Bum."[12] And Croswell Bowen described this persisting aspect of the man as "The Black Irishman."[13] O'Neill possessed (or was possessed by) three different selves. The first was rebellious, violent, and often drunken. The second was the dedicated creative artist. The third was the compassionate "great spirit" who understood human tragedy because he himself had lived it.

These same three selves (or conflicting but complementary aspects of the single Self) were personified long ago as the three chief gods of Hinduism: Shiva, the god of destruction; Brahma, the god of creation; and Vishnu, the god of preservation. In the Elephanta Caves near Bombay a giant statue still stands, whose massive head is carved with the three separate faces of this triune God. First is the scowling face of Shiva, the destroyer; second, the impassive face of Brahma, the creator; third, the compassionate face of Vishnu, the preserver.

Like the mysterious East which he always idealized, O'Neill's character included these three "faces," or selves. Each of these dominated one of the three periods of his life. His youth was naturally violent, rebellious, and destructive. But about 1916, when he suddenly achieved success with his plays, he began a "new life." From 1916 to about 1932 he devoted himself exclusively to the creation of his dramas, and during this period spent himself on his labor of creation. Then, from 1932 to 1945, he retired into himself, brooded upon the life of his nation and of his family, and produced the compassionate autobiographical dramas of his final years.

Because each of the three periods of his life was dominated by a different self (or set of motives, or way of life), it was natural that his emotional needs during each period should have been different. And although his relations with women were never simple—during his youth his affairs often seemed wholly promiscuous—his emotional life followed essentially the same pattern as his professional life. A violent hostility toward women characterized his youth, and the first play he wrote (while still in the sanitarium) was ironically entitled *A Wife for a Life*, and it concluded with the hero's wife running off with the hero's best friend. Clearly O'Neill never believed that marriages were made in heaven, but he always was fascinated by the complex psychological problems of love and marriage.

The actual pattern of his own three marriages may fairly be described, without irony, as "Three Wives for Three Lives." Because the first period of his life was rebellious and destructive, his first marriage was hardly a marriage at all. His first wife was, figuratively, an image of purity who existed in order to be destroyed. His second wife naturally became the opposite—an image of love unlimited, herself an artist, beyond convention and beyond society. But, as he became famous and as he became older, he needed to be protected both from society and from his own weaknesses. Therefore his third wife became an image of worldly sophistication. His three wives satisfied the needs of his three lives.

O'Neill early described his first marriage, in a letter to his first biographer, as "a mistake." He never lived with Kathleen Jenkins, his first wife, and apparently he never even believed that he loved her. Like the semi-autobiographical hero of *The Straw*, he had persuaded a nice girl that he loved her; she became pregnant; he married her. He had, as it were, admitted his legal responsibility, but he then rejected all social responsibility by leaving for Honduras. And his young wife in time accepted the situation: three years later, with his active cooperation, she obtained a divorce.

The character of Kathleen Jenkins (the little we know of it) seems as symbolic as their marriage was formal. "She had big blue eyes, and fair hair piled high on her head. . . . At twenty, Kathleen resembled the lovely girls Charles Dana Gibson was drawing."[14] The daughter of a rich New York businessman, she suggests the imaginary, pure heroine of *The Hairy Ape*, to whose world of high society the primitive Yank could never "belong." But in actuality it was O'Neill who rejected the formal, social world of Kathleen Jenkins—not the pure heroine who rejected the rough physical world of the hero. O'Neill's first marriage was destroyed by his sense of the abyss between the world of

American actuality and the formal world of American society, and by his identification with the former. In youth he followed the flesh, admitting only the formal demands of society. In later years he observed wonderingly that "the woman I gave the most trouble to has given me the least." The clear reason was that this first marriage had never been more than a matter of form.

Seven years later he had spent his *wanderjahre*—in Honduras, on the high seas, in Buenos Aires, and in the cities of America. He had tried his hand at many trades, and succeeded in none. He had suffered a physical breakdown from tuberculosis and from too much drinking. But most important, he had begun writing plays, and had already gained recognition with them: his early one-acters had been produced by the Provincetown Players. And in the fall of 1917 he was living in Greenwich Village, sharing the bohemian life of the leading artists of the time. There he met another young writer, Agnes Boulton. They fell immediately in love, and six months later they married.

Agnes Boulton was almost the exact opposite of Kathleen Jenkins. Not only was she an artist, but the daughter of an artist. Her father was a portrait painter, and she had recently come to New York to earn her living as a free-lance writer. Like O'Neill, she also had been married and had had a child. She was twenty-four years old; he, twenty-nine. They shared friends and a common background. Before their marriage he had already quarreled with and insulted her, and she had recognized his violent nature and accepted it. Neither of them expected conventional behavior of the other, or a conventional life together. Most significantly, they had agreed that, whenever either of them wished, the marriage would be dissolved. The form was nothing; love, everything.

This second marriage was one of equals, not of opposites. But, of course, it was also a marriage of individuals, with individual differences. Agnes, a writer, regarded writing as a business, not an ideal—her work was published in the pulp magazines. She admired his work, and read and praised much of it in manuscript; but she did not care for the theater, and never bothered to make his theater friends her own. He inscribed his first major drama to her "in memory of the wonderful moment when first in your eyes I saw the promise of a land more beautiful than any I had ever known . . . a land beyond my horizon." And for many years they explored together the beauty of this impossible land of romance. For almost a decade they lived together—not always happily, but always creatively. During this marriage to Agnes Boulton he wrote the plays that made him famous and that established him as "our greatest dramatist."

To O'Neill the dramatist, Agnes Boulton's greatest fault was that she wanted to be a separate human individual, not merely the wife of a great man. Like the heroine of *Welded*, she asked: "Haven't I a right to myself as you have to yourself?" Although O'Neill the man agreed, the creative dramatist demanded a more selfless love. When the playwright hid himself away in his study of write, his wife went out with friends, or invited them to visit. When he came out of hiding to join them, she did nothing to protect him from his alcoholism, but drank happily with him. After his sessions with a psychiatrist in New York, during which he determined to end his drinking, he also determined to end his marriage to Agnes Boulton. He had grown to need protection and the nurture of his genius, not domestic love and comradeship.

During the summer and fall of 1926, he began seeing a good deal of Carlotta Monterey. A mutual friend of the time described her as "miraculously immaculate, and a wonderful housekeeper. There was nobody like her. Agnes' house, on the other hand, always seemed to smell of diapers and lamb stew, and there was always a lot of noise from the kids. [Shane had been born in 1919, Oona in 1925.] It drove O'Neill almost out of his mind."[15] O'Neill himself casually wrote to a friend about "Carlotta Monterey, the famous beauty." This combination of immaculate housekeeper and famous beauty was what the creative artist now needed. "One day he came to tea," Carlotta remembered, ". . . and he looked at me with those tragic eyes and said, 'I need you.' He kept saying 'I need you, I need you'—never 'I love you, I think you are wonderful'—just 'I need you, I need you.' Sometimes it was a bit frightening."[16] Although such compelling love was always to remain a bit frightening, she accepted her destiny.

Actually Carlotta Monterey and Eugene O'Neill had met four years earlier when she was acting the role of the immaculate heroine of *The Hairy Ape*. He had scarcely noticed her then, and he had not seen her again until 1926; but there seems to have been something prophetic about her early role. She had interpreted with theatrical skill the character of that beautiful but unreal heroine—a character whom the innocence of his first wife had perhaps suggested. And then gradually, she herself had realized this beautiful immaculateness in her own life. By her mimetic art she had created—in the phrase of Henry James— "the real thing." By falling in love with her, therefore, O'Neill was falling in love with the actualization of an ideal image which his fantasy had earlier created. In marrying her, he was marrying both an immaculate housekeeper and an ideal beauty.

The character of Carlotta Monterey is, indeed, almost as complex as that of O'Neill himself. She was not "really" even "Carlotta Monterey": she had been born Hazel Neilson Tharsing, and she had grown up in the unglamorous surroundings of Oakland, dreaming of becoming an actress. She had then adopted a stage name to suggest the glamour and the aristocracy (a little removed, both in time and in space) of the Spanish past of her California home. Gradually she had molded herself in the image of this aristocratic ideal. She had described herself as convent-bred and Continent-educated. She had never become widely famous as an actress, but she had become a famous beauty. Already married three times, she had become independently wealthy. She had become, that is, infinitely more than the simple ideal of immaculate beauty which O'Neill had imagined earlier to contrast with his Hairy Ape. She had become America's ideal of aristocratic grace and worldly success, and she was the perfect creature to nurture the genius of America's greatest dramatist.

But for more than two years O'Neill was denied the opportunity for undisturbed work which his marriage to Carlotta promised, because of the difficulties (both emotional and financial) created by the refusal of Agnes to a quick divorce. Meanwhile, he and Carlotta embarked on a long voyage to the Orient—and to his old dream of perfect Beauty beyond the horizon. But suddenly the dream exploded into a nightmare: the tension involved in their unsanctioned relationship drove O'Neill to one last drunken escape, which ended in a Shanghai hospital. After his recovery, the couple returned to Europe. And finally on July 22, 1929, two days after Agnes was granted her divorce in Reno, he and Carlotta were married in Paris.

For sixteen years this third marriage brought him what peace and happiness his restless nature would allow. On their twelfth wedding anniversary he dedicated the recently completed manuscript of *Long Day's Journey* to Carlotta, with the inscription: "These twelve years, Beloved One, have been a Journey into Light—and love." But his health had become increasingly bad, and finally the diagnosis of Parkinson's disease destroyed hope of recovery. After 1944, he lost all power to work creatively.

This final loss of creative power naturally resulted in increasing frustration, which almost caused the break-up of his third marriage. While he had been writing the later plays, Carlotta had acted as protector and guardian of his talents: she had kept away reporters and unwanted visitors; she had shielded him both from the temptations of the world and of his own nature. But in 1946, when he found himself unable to work, he suddenly threw himself into new activities. He participated actively in the production of *The Iceman Cometh*. And beyond this professional activity, he suddenly found new pleasure in social relationships, both with old friends and with new acquaintances. For the first time he allowed himself to enjoy the vanities of being a literary lion. And he also began flirting happily with young actresses and secretaries. But Carlotta, jealous both of new acquaintances and of old friends, and no longer able to control or to protect him, became increasingly disturbed. Finally, she deserted him. Both suffered complete physical and nervous breakdowns, and ironically both were treated in the same hospital. They recovered, and were finally reconciled. But during the last years the light, which had shone on the third stage of the long journey, faded.

The final tragedy which darkened his last years, preventing him from enjoying the rewards of his labors and calling down final doom on the house of O'Neill, was caused by the same conflicts that had troubled his earlier years. Carlotta had married him to protect him from interruption by noisy children and by sociable friends. Now when, unable to work, he needed the companionship of children and friends, she still protected him. Increasingly, he had sought to renew contacts with Eugene, Jr., and with Shane and Oona. But Oona offended Carlotta by her gay irreverence, and, when she married Charlie Chaplin (a close friend of Carlotta's last husband, and a man as old as her father), O'Neill disowned her. Shane had already suffered from the family curse of drink and dope. But Eugene, Jr., had achieved success as a scholar, and he had won his father's admiration and affection. But his radical politics, much like his father's in youth, offended Carlotta, and the father was forced to choose between wife and son. He chose Carlotta, and Eugene, Jr., committed suicide. Tragedy became O'Neill.

VI *Autobiography and Tragedy*

From 1913, when he began writing his first play while still in the sanitarium, to 1920, when his first full-length drama was produced on Broadway, O'Neill wrote many plays of many different types. Most of these were apprentice pieces which have been mercifully forgotten; and, in this brief introduction, we shall not have space to consider most of them. But the reasons for their failures are significant: they illuminate the nature both of his life and of his writing.

It has often been said that O'Neill was an autobiographical writer—and the tremendous success of *Long Day's Journey* and the other final dramas seems to confirm this. In following his early life, we have also followed the autobiographical story of *Long Day's Journey,* even when his actual life diverged from it. But it is important to remember that the major autobiographical plays were all written toward the end of his career; for in his early life, his best plays were not autobiographical: *The Emperor Jones,* for instance, is one of the least autobiographical plays in literature. Successful autobiography requires insight into the nature of the "hero" and perspective upon his actions and his relationships with the world; but, throughout his early life, O'Neill emphatically lacked this insight. He possessed a keen power of observation of the people about him, and an extraordinary insight into the characters and motives of others; but the more of himself he incorporated into his early characters, the more confused they became; the more turgid was the style of his writing; and the more distorted was the pattern of his dramas. Only as he matured as an artist and playwright was he able to utilize successfully the subjective experiences of his early years: with the slow passage of time he achieved perspective and self-knowledge.

The failure of his early autobiographical plays is interesting. Each creates successful minor characters and physical settings of great verisimilitude. But in each the central character remains unconvincing. The autobiographical hero seems to be an abstract idea, a sentimental projection, or an idealized symbol. Throughout his early career O'Neill succeeded only when he dramatized objective characters whom he had observed, or when he projected the conflicting aspects of his own inner nature as separate, conflicting protagonists upon the stage.

The first play which he ever wrote was the brief skit entitled *A Wife for a Life*. It ended: "Greater love hath no man than this that he giveth his wife for a friend." And the savage sarcasm (or, perhaps, the maudlin sentimentality) of this final speech reflected the emotional confusion of his own nature at the time. It recalled not only the recent destruction of his own first marriage, but also the confusion of his own love affair with Louise Bryant, the wife of his friend John Reed. This play failed for many reasons, but chiefly because of the author's lack of objectivity toward his characters and their situation.

Later O'Neill attempted to dramatize the story of his own attempted suicide in *Exorcism*. Written in 1919 and produced in 1920, the play was never published. But Alexander Woollcott reviewed it favorably, and commented particularly on the excellence of the minor characters. The hero remained less convincing, however, because the play first described his suicide-attempt as a farce, but then asserted baldly the hero's conviction that he had succeeded in "exorcising" his self-destructive former self. The first of O'Neill's plays to deal with the crucial year 1912 and to attempt to dramatize the transformation of the irresponsible beachcomber into the future tragic artist, it asserted this magical transformation too abstractly, and it did not describe the tragic motives behind it. Therefore the complex character of the hero remained an idealized projection of his true self.

The Straw, written at about the same time as *Exorcism*, and produced one year later, went on to describe the young hero's experiences in a tuberculosis sanitarium. Again, the minor characters, such as the nurses and doctors, are excellent, and the background realistic. The hero, Stephen Murray, seems an almost exact dramatization of the author: he is a former newspaper reporter who is inspired to write serious literature during his stay at the sanitarium and who finds in this vocation a new reason for living. Furthermore, this Stephen conducts a romance with a fellow-patient, just as the young O'Neill actually did. But the character of Stephen Murray is romanticized far beyond the actual young O'Neill, and the play is provided with a sentimental ending to fit. Stephen realizes that his romantic attentions have caused the tubercular heroine to fall seriously in love with him, and the doctor tells him that her only hope of recovery lies in his love. Nobly, therefore, he proclaims to her his true love and asks her to marry him, and he discovers in the process that he actually loves her. She happily accepts, and together they grasp at "the straw" of hope which this romantic love provides. The play ends sadly in the shadow of the heroine's probable death, but it ends "happily" with the triumph of true love over death.

Stephen Murray of *The Straw* is the typical romantic hero whom the young O'Neill constructed out of the materials of his own early biography. His discovery of his true vocation as a creative writer while recuperating in the sanitarium is both actual and romantically ideal. But, except in this one aspect, O'Neill himself was never a romantic hero. Unlike the fictional hero of *The Straw*, he never proclaimed his true love to the actual patient at "Gaylord Farm" with whom he conducted his romance and who died soon after leaving the sanitarium without ever seeing him again. Eugene O'Neill was a much less romantic —and a much more complicated—person than his fictional hero. Indeed, he did project something of his own complexity upon Stephen Murray, in his stage directions: "His manner, as revealed by his speech—nervous, inquisitive, alert—seems more an acquired quality than any part of his true nature." But in the play, this conflict between "acquired quality" and "true nature" is re-solved in the romantic heroism of the ending. In O'Neill's actual life, the inner conflict was never fully resolved. The play both sentimentalized and oversimplified the reality.

The last early play to describe and interpret autobiographically the experiences of the young O'Neill is *Welded*. Completed in 1923 and four years after *The Straw*, it deals with the emotional problems of his second marriage as he was then experiencing them. It marks an interesting advance over the others in con-ception of character and theme, but there is also an interesting regression in the use of dialogue and emotional tone. The character of its autobiographical hero is much more complex and true to life than in *Exorcism* and *The Straw*; and the conflict described —both psychologically, within the hero's mind and dramatically, between husband and wife—is more interesting. But the dialogue is always rhetorical and it is often incredible: the emotion is so overstrained that it seldom falls below the level of hysteria. The play also fails because it attempts too much too soon: the deep probing of character and the dramatic analysis of emotion—which were to contribute to the later successes of *Strange Interlude* and of *Mourning Becomes Electra*—resulted only in psychological melodrama.

Michael Cape, the hero of *Welded* (O'Neill's English publisher was named Jonathan Cape), is a successful playwright who is almost exactly the author's age at the time of writing: "His unusual face is a harrowed battleground of super-sensitiveness, the features at war with one another. . . . There is something tortured about him—a passionate tension. . . ." The stage description of his wife, Eleanor, exactly fits O'Neill's second wife, Agnes Boulton, in age and physical appearance, although Eleanor is an "actress," whereas Agnes was a novelist. O'Neill projected upon the fictional Michael and Eleanor Cape the fundamental conflicts of his own life: the universal conflict (always present in his mind) between romantic love and work-a-day reality; and the more personal conflict (then becoming acute in his experience) between "our greatest playwright," dedicated only to his art, and the passionate human being in need of love, but exclusively centered upon himself and his own problems.

The failure of *Welded*—unlike the earlier autobiographical dramas—is caused partly by the lack of realism in the minor characters and in the background. These characters are no longer actual people, but symbols: the other man is, simply, "John," a theatrical producer, and the other woman is, even more simply, "A Woman." This symbolism is emphasized by the stage directions: *"two circles of light, like auras of egotism, emphasize Eleanor and Michael throughout the play. There is no other lighting. The two other people and the rooms are distinguishable only by the light of Eleanor and Michael."* The realism, however, is now transferred to the emotional life of the husband

and wife who quarrel violently, rush off to seek solace from others, and return to make up passionately; they follow the pattern which five years later was to destroy O'Neill's own second marriage. The lack of verisimilitude in these autobiographical characters is caused by the exaggerated intensity of their dialogue and, finally, by the happy ending. Once again love romantically conquers all:

> Cape. (*leaping to his feet—intensely*) My own!
> Eleanor. (*with deep, passionate tenderness*) My lover!
> Cape. My wife! (*His eyes fixed on her, he ascends . . .*)

The young O'Neill used his own experiences to project upon the stage the inner conflicts which were tormenting him. In *Exorcism* he did not really try to understand these conflicts. In *The Straw* he dramatized the problems, but he romanticized the autobiographical hero and also the ending. In *Welded* he realized both the problems and the true character of the hero, but he melodramatized them and once again projected an impossibly romantic ending. All these plays failed dismally. But, meanwhile, he often succeeded brilliantly when he projected his inner conflicts upon opposing dramatic characters like Robert and Andrew Mayo of *Beyond the Horizon*. And meanwhile, in actual life, he sought by means of reading, discussion, and reflection to understand his own conflicts and those of all men.
∠ More than most creative writers, O'Neill concerned himself with the inner thoughts and feelings of his protagonists and of himself⟩ Many of his greatest successes explored and dramatized this inner world. Therefore, psychologists and psychoanalysts have been deeply interested in his dramas, and many critics have emphasized the psychoanalytic nature of all his writing.[17] Negatively, he has often been criticized for excessive introversion and for conscious borrowing from the theories of Freud and of Jung. But the facts do not fully substantiate this criticism. Just as his use of autobiographical material was at first tentative and unsuccessful, so was his interest in—and use of—analytical psychology.

O'Neill early disclaimed any specific interest in Freud, and there is no reason to doubt his statement. But he did affirm an enthusiasm for Carl Jung: "Some of his suggestions I find extraordinarily illuminating in the light of my own experience with hidden motives." He particularly liked Jung's theory of the "collective unconscious," and of the archetypal patterns and myths which precede conscious thought and literary creation. As early as 1922 O'Neill used this theory to explain his preference for emotion over conscious thought: "Our emotions . . . are the result not only of our individual experience, but of the experiences of the human race back through the ages."[18] But the more specific "complexes" and the more intellectual analyses of Freud seemed to him too mechanical. When he adapted elements of the Oedipus story in *Desire Under the Elms,* he produced (as Dr. Weissman has described it) "unconscious autobiography."

But in 1926 O'Neill underwent six weeks of psychological analysis by Dr. Gilbert Hamilton of New York City, for the specific, practical purpose of curing his alcoholism (which was successfully cured). Although not extended enough or deep enough to be called a true psychoanalysis, these psychiatric interviews served both to clarify some of his own problems and to interest him more deeply in Freudian psychology. And this interest found dramatic expression in *Strange Interlude,* which he wrote soon after. This play, certainly the most consciously psychological of all, has often been criticized for its Freudian jargon and for its self-conscious theorizing. Yet even in it the fundamental emotional experiences dramatized and the psychological interpretations suggested were taken from the author's own earlier experience and observation more than from mere Freudian theory, as his recent biographers have made clear. His extraordinarily intense personal experiences and his extraordinarily acute sympathy with the emotional problems of all people contributed more to his tragic psychology than did Freudian theory—he was not being pretentious when he wrote earlier of "my own experience with hidden motives."

In one sense, all of O'Neill's dramatic art is autobiographical, for it is directed toward the understanding of his own life and of his inner "self." But in a truer sense, his unresolved inner conflicts, which troubled him throughout his life, stirred his imagination to dramatize the conflicts of all men, and, ultimately, to clarify his own.

Perhaps the contemporaneity of O'Neill and his plays is to blame: we are so close to him that we know too much about his life. It is interesting to speculate what our interpretation of Shakespeare might be today if we knew as many facts of his biography as we do of O'Neill's. Shakespeare also married young, deserted his wife, ran off to join a troupe of actors, and eventually wrote plays about the tragic problems of troubled men such as Hamlet and Othello. We can only infer the personal conflicts of the artists of earlier times. But O'Neill's personal conflicts are public knowledge.

VII "Our Greatest Dramatist"

O'Neill's public and professional life was as orderly, responsible, and reasonable as his early private life had been disorderly, irresponsible, and unreasonable. The playwright always listened to serious criticism, and he learned from his professional mistakes. His relations with producers and actors were better than those of most authors. In later years, remembering the difficulties and discouragements of his own early career, he took pains to write encouraging letters to younger men whose work he admired. To readers and critics who sincerely wished to understand and discuss his art, he was unfailingly gracious. Many of the greatest writers of his time offered him their ungrudging admiration. From his first meeting with George Jean Nathan, he enjoyed the lifelong friendship of the leading theatrical critic of his time. And Theodore Drieser, who respected few men, stood in awe of O'Neill.

The disagreements which sometimes troubled his professional career were always reasonable. He judged his own work—and all criticisms of it—by one unfailing standard: did it attempt to realize the highest principles of art and literature? Or did it cater to the popular demands of the commercial theater? The paternal shadow of "The Count of Monte Cristo" hung over his professional career. With all critics and producers who expected conformity to the commercial standards that had determined his father's career, he quarreled. But he accepted all criticisms of his work which appealed to the highest standards of art. His own earliest recorded critical judgment is typical. Professor George Pierce Baker had invited the opinions of his students concerning an apprentice work which he had just read aloud, and other classmates had given their careful criticisms.

But O'Neill simply commented: "Cut it to twenty minutes, give it a couple of tunes, and it's sure fire burly-cue." If he thought that he detected elements of the "phony" or of the merely theatrical in his own writing (as he often did—for he was, inevitably, his father's son), he rejected them. For this reason he grew to dislike some of his own most popular early plays such as *In the Zone* and *Anna Christie*. And for the same reason he perhaps overvalued his most experimental, original plays, such as *The Great God Brown.*

But from childhood he had been brought up with the practical realities of the theater. Besides experiences with his father's troupe, he enjoyed the advice of some of his father's friends. When his first volume of plays was published, critic Clayton Hamilton praised it publicly but privately warned the young playwright: "When you send off a play remember there is not one chance in a thousand it will ever be read; not one chance in a million of its ever being accepted—(and if accepted it will probably never be produced). . . ." And for two years O'Neill wrote steadily but unsuccessfully.

In 1916, however, he achieved sudden success. From John Reed and Louise Bryant he had heard of the recently organized little theater group called the Provincetown Players, and in early summer he packed up "a trunk-full of plays" and moved to Provincetown. There he offered the manuscript of *Bound East for Cardiff* to the group, where it was read aloud. Later Susan Glaspell remembered the occasion: "Then we knew what we were for. . . . I may see it through memories too emotional, but it seems to me I have never sat before a more moving production than our *Bound East for Cardiff*." And from this first production he was to go on from success to greater success. Contrasting with the tragic story of his private life, his public life became a story of brilliant success.

During the summer of 1916 he continued to write and to work with the Provincetown group. He himself acted in *Thirst,* his second play to be produced. And in the fall, when they all returned to New York, *Bound East for Cardiff* featured the opening bill at the Playwright's Theatre. His father and mother, who came to see it were pleased. Critical reviews were enthusiastic, and gradually word spread that Eugene O'Neill was a new playwright to be watched. Other one-act plays of his were soon produced, and, by the second summer at Province-town, he had already become something of a legend. The most remarkable aspect of his reputation, both then and later, has been the extreme respect with which he has been regarded by his peers. An old friend of his newspaper days on the New London *Telegraph*, who joined him that summer in Provincetown, was astonished at the veneration with which he was already re-garded: "Here's the great new American playwright in the making," they said; and few disagreed.

One of the first full-length articles to discuss the new play-wright was published by George Jean Nathan in 1920, and it included some severe criticism with its praise. O'Neill wrote Nathan to thank him and also "to make you my confession of faith. . . . My work is as yet a mere groping. I rate myself a beginner—with prospects. . . . But I venture to promise that this will be less true with each succeeding play. . . . And in this faith I live: That if I have the 'guts' to ignore the megaphone men and what goes with them, to follow the dream and live for that alone, then my real significant bit of truth, and the ability to express it, will be conquered in time."[19] Not only did this modest prophecy prove true, but it won Nathan over completely. Even when the two men later disagreed—as they did concerning the merits of *Lazarus Laughed*—they completely respected each other.

When O'Neill's first full-length play was produced in New York, it won immediate acclaim. At first produced experimentally, *Beyond the Horizon* soon moved to a regular run in a large Broadway theater. James O'Neill, who was able to attend it six months before his death, took great pleasure in his son's success. Soon it won the Pulitzer Prize. If some critics objected to its alternations of scenes and if James O'Neill registered his usual objections to its tragic tone, the success of the play seemed all the more remarkable for these very reasons. It went against the theatrical conventions and against the popular taste of the time. It inaugurated a new era in the American theater—one which is still continuing a half century later.

Within the year *The Emperor Jones* was produced in New York. It followed the same pattern as its predecessor, but won a wider success and a greater acclaim; for both its subject matter and its technique appealed beyond the limits of the American theater to the imagination of the world. The story of the West Indian Negro "emperor" had the universal appeal of folk myth, and its theatrical presentation seemed both more imaginative and more elemental than that of *Beyond the Horizon*. It established O'Neill as an international figure. And even today, if American drama is discussed in Tokyo or in Buenos Aires, *The Emperor Jones* is apt to be the first play mentioned.

One year later O'Neill's third major play won his second Pulitzer Prize. And it appealed to a type of audience less attracted to his earlier plays. For *Anna Christie*, with its story of the regeneration of a "fallen woman," its romantic sentiment, and its un-tragic ending, seemed closer to popular taste. Like *Ah, Wilderness!* and *Strange Interlude* later, it appealed to an American middle class which rather disliked pure tragedy and distrusted art for art's sake. Fifteen years later, when Bernard De Voto wrote his "Minority Report" disapproving of the award of the Nobel Prize to O'Neill, he singled out *Anna Christie* for praise. But O'Neill, because he always distrusted popular acclaim and sentimental success, soon turned against *Anna*.

His fourth major success within two years, *The Hairy Ape*, introduced a new aspect of the author's genius. Modeled after the new "expressionistic" drama, it first employed those techniques of anti-realism, or "super-naturalism," which his later plays were to develop—the conscious use of symbolism, the use of masks, and other techniques which would suggest the sharp division between surface reality and the subconscious mind. Like *The Great God Brown* and *Strange Interlude*, this play was aggressively experimental; and it seemed, therefore, to challenge the imagination of its audiences. And again, both its title and its subject matter appealed beyond the national audience to the international. With *The Hairy Ape* O'Neill achieved new success without repeating himself in any way, and he established himself as a tragic dramatist of international stature.

Only three years after the production of his first full-length play, and on the basis of only four major successes, his reputation had achieved unprecedented heights: he was universally recognized as "America's greatest dramatist." But this recognition meant comparatively little at a time when America had produced no major dramatists. The extent of his international reputation was more remarkable. Writing in *Dublin Magazine* in 1923, an Irish critic could dare to rank O'Neill above the greatest playwrights of the time: "Eugene O'Neill is the great discovery of the post-war drama. His is the star now in the ascendant, outshining Shaw, Synge. . . . and all the Continentals."[20] There were dissenting voices, then as always; but the depth, the breadth, and the genuine literary quality of the enthusiasm which these early dramas aroused was astonishing. And, as his new plays continued to appear throughout the decade, this early reputation continued to grow and to spread.

As O'Neill became famous, he became not only increasingly conscious of his public position but also increasingly articulate about his ideals and hopes for American drama. Moreover, his new sense of public responsibility found expression both in his writing and in his relations with producers. From the beginning, he had identified himself with the experimental theater of the Provincetown Players; now he wrote frequent letters—both to his friends and to the newspapers—to describe his ideas and hopes for the modern drama. Some of these ideas he derived from his associates—as from *The Theatre of Tomorrow* by Kenneth Macgowan.[21] Others he developed from Nietzsche, Strindberg, and contemporary dramatists. But he made these ideas his own, and he gave them concrete expression in his plays from *Beyond the Horizon* to *Lazarus Laughed*. Always he emphasized his idealistic, anti-naturalistic—and, indeed, optimistic—belief that all tragic drama is essentially religious in origin and in effect. But inevitably this high conception of the drama brought him into conflict with the practical-minded producers of his time.

Having achieved fame, O'Neill now achieved notoriety. His next plays suffered attacks from the censors—*All God's Chillun,* for its racial theme; *Desire,* for its "immorality." Although these attacks were largely unjustified, other plays of this period suffered criticism (and sometimes failure) for better reasons. *The Fountain* and *Welded* both asserted his idealistic theories without the necessary dramatic conviction. When regular producers refused them, O'Neill formed his own company with Kenneth Macgowan and Robert E. Jones, and he personally produced them; but both inevitably failed. But *The Great God Brown* succeeded. However, his finest drama of ideas, *Lazarus*

Laughed, proved both too expensive and too idealistic to produce commercially. By 1927 he had achieved fame sufficient to convince the Theatre Guild that it should produce almost any new play of his. And, at the same time, he had exhausted the missionary idealism which had impelled him to write plays which had proved either impracticable or undramatic.

With the production of *Strange Interlude* in 1928, his reputation reached new heights. Some critics hailed the drama with superlatives, and Nathan devoted a complete article to praising it. But even more remarkable was the sheer physical triumph of the production, which ran continuously for more than a year, even though each performance lasted for five hours (with an hour off for dinner). Three years later, when the trilogy of *Mourning Becomes Electra* repeated this triumph, O'Neill's name was often mentioned with the immortals. In 1929 an Australian critic, who had written a book about O'Neill's plays, compared him with Shakespeare. And now his modern dramatization of the Greek Oresteia challenged comparison with Aeschylus. Many objected to such *lèse majesté,* and later criticism has often dealt harshly with these ambitious plays. But their historical success was both undeniable and unparalleled.

The next years proved less successful. And after 1934 O'Neill's retirement from active playwriting, which was to continue for twelve years, worked against his earlier reputation. When he received the Nobel Prize for literature in 1936, many articles were devoted to assessing his past achievement. These articles were mostly favorable, of course. But now that he had received the highest accolade possible, it seemed appropriate to call his whole work into question, and many critics repeated their earlier doubts with greater emphasis. And their critical attacks, combined with his own continued retirement and professional silence, undermined his reputation.

Moreover, O'Neill's decade of silence between the award of the Nobel Prize in 1936 and the production of *The Iceman Cometh* in 1946 was dominated by two historical events which worked powerfully against his reputation. The era of the Great Depression was followed by that of World War II, and these twin disasters seemed to provide in actual life enough tragedy to blunt men's taste for dramatic tragedy. O'Neill had earlier planned to write a tragedy to follow *Dynamo* in which "gold" was to supplant the "dynamo" as the modern "god"; but (as he phrased it in a letter) "the Great Depression caught up with its prophecies,"[22] and he abandoned it. From the point of view of the pragmatic critics of the time, his tragic dramas criticizing the materialism of American life seemed almost treasonous. Of O'Neill and his colleagues it was charged: "They Turned Their Backs on America." In complete physical and spiritual retirement at "Tao House," O'Neill sat out the depression and World War II, and his reputation suffered.

At the end of the war he moved to New York to supervise the production of *The Iceman Cometh* by the Theatre Guild in 1946. But this play, on which he had pinned great hopes, achieved only moderate success. And shortly thereafter *A Moon for the Misbegotten* closed without reaching Broadway. Perhaps the mood of the American public remained too preoccupied with war to be ready for these tragedies. Or perhaps these tragedies introduced a new technique of ironic ambivalence for which the audiences of the time were not ready. But, whatever the reason, O'Neill failed to recover his former eminence. Until his death in 1953 he lived in unhappy retirement while younger dramatists usurped the spotlight. No one seriously questioned his title as "our greatest dramatist." But at his death the obituary notices seemed somewhat retrospective and elegiac.

In 1956, however, following the production of *Long Day's Journey*, a sudden revival of his reputation occurred. The tremendous acclaim that greeted this play was both immediate and international in scope; but its single importance is easily overestimated. Even more important was the revival in this same year of *The Iceman* and its astonishing success with critics and audiences. It was as if a new theater-going public had suddenly rediscovered an old playwright and as if a younger generation had decided that O'Neill's genius belonged to it also. Following these successes *A Moon* was finally produced on Broadway, and *A Touch of the Poet* enjoyed a long run a year later. Meanwhile, books about the playwright began coming from the presses, and this modern revival of a reputation apparently dead seemed almost as incredible as the revival of Lazarus.

But before this sudden, native revival of O'Neill's fame in 1956, a more gradual growth of interest and acclaim had been evident abroad. America's greatest dramatist had long been held in greater esteem on the Continent than at home, and the decade from 1952 to 1962 saw the publication in foreign languages of six full-length books about his plays—more studies than in English. In Sweden his final plays were produced prior to their Broadway openings, and Karl-Ragnar Gierow, director of the Royal Dramatic Theatre of Stockholm, was personally responsible for the first production of *Long Day's Journey*. American literary history abounds in examples of the neglect of its authors by domestic audiences until foreign appreciation focuses attention on them. But O'Neill's case was somewhat different. Early recognized and acclaimed as "our greatest dramatist," he was later neglected. But after his death new acclaim from abroad re-established his reputation as one of the major dramatists of the modern world.

VIII   *"More Stately Mansions"*

Throughout his career O'Neill wrote serious tragedies and renounced the easy, commercial success of dramas such as *The Count of Monte Cristo*. These tragedies denounced American materialism and often satirized the acquisitiveness of the business-man. But, even while renouncing the success which his father had achieved, and even while attacking American materialism, O'Neill progressively achieved that very financial success against which he inveighed. The greatest irony in a life filled with ironies was this seemingly unsought material success. Not only did he achieve quick popular and critical acclaim in a particular-ly difficult and unpopular profession, but he also achieved spectacular financial success in a profession devoted to the denunciation of financial success. Much of the shrewd mate-rialism of Marco Millions and Billy Brown seemed to lurk just under the sensitive skin of the tragic author.

In his youth he had always shared the expensive tastes of the young man about town, and had desired the money to satisfy them (which his father had refused to provide). But, for a long period following his years before the mast, he identified himself with sailors, and he often dressed in a cheap sailor's jersey and cap. During his apprenticeship to the writing profession, his bohemian friends naturally discouraged any taste for elegance. And his second wife never cared much for appearances. But gradually, as his serious plays achieved financial success, his scale of living grew to approximate that of his father. *In the Zone,* one of his earliest plays of the sea, earned a small but steady income because of its long run in vaudeville. When *Beyond the Horizon* won his first Pulitzer Prize, he seemed unexcited at first; but, when he learned of the financial award involved: "I practically went delirious! I was broke or nearly. A thousand dollars was sure a thousand dollars!" And as success followed success, he continued to value the money as much—if not more—than the fame. He moved progressively up the scale of luxurious living, from a Provincetown cabin, to a country farm, to a Bermuda mansion. When his most spectacular attack on materialism proved most spectacularly successful on Broadway, he cheered it on: "Come on, you 'Brown'! Daddy needs a yacht!"[23]

The irony of his materialistic success was obvious, but it seems not to have troubled him at first. And his lifelong devotion to tragedy remained genuine—never did he compromise consciously with the high standards of his art, nor resort to the potboilers with which so many serious writers have pieced out their meager incomes. O'Neill continued to write pure tragedies, whether or not they succeeded financially. And the first half of his career concluded with his most unrelieved and purely literary tragedy—*Mourning Becomes Electra.* This major work did not succeed very well financially. But he had already achieved financial self-sufficiency.

During the period following his separation from his second wife and ending with his marriage to his third, a gradual change in his habits occurred. He had left Agnes partly because she was a careless bohemian and a poor housekeeper; he married Carlotta partly because she was an excellent housekeeper who could (and would) regulate his irregular life. But Carlotta loved elegance and luxury as Agnes never had, and to please her he learned to live and to dress elegantly. A photograph of the time shows him standing in a topcoat, with a silk scarf and kid gloves, grinning self-consciously as he holds his fedora delicately with his fingertips. And his first home with Carlotta was a forty-five room chateau at Saint Antoine du Rocher, where they lived for two years. He had achieved the ultimate in financial and social success; but he seemed increasingly uneasy about it.

His uneasiness at his own spectacular affluence was reinforced by two events. In 1928 he had traveled with Carlotta to the Orient which he had always idealized, but he had been appalled by its poverty and starvation. Then, after their return to France and their establishment in the chateau, the Great Depression began. Although it did not seriously curtail his income, it increased his pessimism, and it exacerbated his despair at the evils of American materialism. He had already attacked this characteristic in *Dynamo,* and he now struggled to overcome it in *Days Without End.* He had planned a third play about "gold," which he now abandoned; but he began a mammoth Cycle attacking the materialism of an Irish-American family, to be entitled "A Tale of Possessors Self-Dispossessed."

The significant quality of all these plays written just before or during the Great Depression is their complete negativism. Materialism is the enemy, but it is also the dominant force in American life. Where Billy Brown and Marco had seemed self-deluded but rather likable villains, these new protagonists were wholly to be condemned, or wholly to be pitied. The very process of "possession" was now described as self-destructive and as resulting ultimately in self-dispossession. Between the romantic self-delusion of the Irish immigrant Cornelius Melody, who still preserved "a touch of the poet," and the materialistic self-delusion of the Yankee family into which his daughter married, O'Neill clearly preferred the romantic poet. But both delusions were hopelessly negative. After O'Neill's failure to find the "secret hidden over there beyond the horizon" in the Orient, and after the Great Depression, his disillusion became absolute.

Of the eleven plays which he planned to constitute his great Cycle, only two have survived; and the second, *More Stately Mansions,* was not published until 1964, although it was produced in Stockholm in 1962, where it was not successful. But its title is richly significant, and its irony is partly autobiographical: the phrase, quoted from "The Chambered Nautilus" by Oliver Wendell Holmes, suggests all the early American idealism which O'Neill and his modern pessimism were now rejecting. "Build thee more stately mansions, O my soul,/As the swift seasons roll!" Holmes had exhorted. And he had emphasized the hopeful idealism: "O my soul!" Now O'Neill, in all his tragic dramas of this period, emphasized only the materialistic American drive: "Build thee more stately mansions."

Following his sojourn in France, during which the unpleasantness of his earlier divorce was gradually forgotten, Eugene and Carlotta returned to New York. And soon they proceeded to build an elaborate new mansion at the fashionable Sea Island Beach, Georgia. His early home in Provincetown had been washed into the sea in 1931, and his second home at "Brook Farm" had been sold; his Bermuda home had been made over to Agnes, and the chateau in France had been rented. Now the luxurious "Casa Genotta" (the name combined "Gene" and "Carlotta") cost $100,000. It featured a large study built to resemble a ship's prow, whose windows faced the Atlantic Ocean over a high protecting wall of stone. It was intended as a sanctuary both for their marriage and for his art. And they referred to it hopefully as "our Blessed Isles," after the romantic sanctuary fondly imagined by the doomed protagonists of *Mourning Becomes Electra*.

But this Georgia mansion proved even less satisfactory than any of his other homes. The Southern heat was enervating, and the new cycle of plays failed to progress. Seeking fresh background for the historic cycle, he traveled to the American Northwest; and there, in 1936, word of his Nobel Prize award reached him. This ultimate proof of international fame marked the high point of his career, and it also brought a cash benefit of $40,000. This money he used—predictably—to build his most stately mansion, "Tao House" in Danville, California.

"Tao House" was as luxurious as his other recent homes; but, from the beginning, it was different. The name invoked a kind of Oriental magic, "Tao" being translated as "the right way of life." It remembered his earlier devotion to Lao-tse and the ancient mystics who had sought to advise "the great Kaan" against the materialism of Marco. And this new house was built to emphasize a new kind of inwardness. Although it faced East across an inland valley toward Mount Diablo, its hall was so designed that the devil's mountain could only be seen reflected in darkened mirrors. And O'Neill's new study was wholly unlike the flamboyant ship's prow of "Casa Genotta"; it was a small grey wood-paneled room, wholly functional. In this study he faced down the ghosts of his own past and wrote his final, autobiographical tragedies.

Concerning Mount Diablo, which the new "Tao House" faced, Californians assert an interesting statistic. They say that the view from the top of the mountain includes a larger area of the earth's surface than can be seen from any other place on earth. This statistic may be true, for Mount Diablo is, technically, a monadnock, and stands high above the neighboring coastal ranges, looking out for two hundred miles across the great Central Valley, north and east and south to Mount Shasta, the Sierra, and the Tehachapis, and looking west beyond the hills of San Francisco to the Pacific horizon. In the past the devil had shown the playwright the kingdoms of the earth, and O'Neill had accepted their material wealth. But now, at last, he retired to the small grey study in the house beneath the devil's mountain to search out his own soul.

The many mansions which O'Neill inhabited during his active life seem also to symbolize the successive stages of his long journey. In an old Coast Guard station perched on the outermost beach of Cape Cod, which he had converted into his first permanent home, he wrote his plays of the sea. In "Brook Farm" at Ridgefield, Connecticut, where the New England elms overhung the old house and its nearby barn, he imagined his *Desire Under the Elms* (while the name, "Brook Farm", ironically recalled the idealism of an earlier New England). In the opulent surroundings of his Bermuda mansion perfectly suited for writing, he created his ideal *Lazarus Laughed* and his giant *Strange Interlude*. In the mannered elegance of a French chateau he composed the intricate acts of his most perfectly designed play, *Mourning Becomes Electra*. Behind the stone walls of "Casa Genotta," he struggled with his most ambitious project for the great American Cycle, but failed. And finally in this new house in the far West facing eastward toward the devil's mountain, he re-invoked the mysticism which he had idealized in youth, but he turned it inward to interpret the tragedies of his early life.

"Build thee more stately mansions, O my soul!" His William A. Brown had been a successful architect, who built luxurious mansions for rich American businessmen. But his Dion Anthony had only been a draftsman who sketched original designs, while hoping to write some great masterpiece. O'Neill himself had built many mansions during his life, but none had ever seemed to realize his dreams. In "Tao House" he looked inward to re-create his own tragic drama. And in this last mansion for his soul, he described the material cause of his tragedy.

In *Long Day's Journey*, Mary Tyrone complained: "I've never felt it was my home." And James Tyrone recalled his anguished hope that, for a moment, "this home has been a home again." At this confession, "*his son looks at him, for the first time with an understanding sympathy. It is as if suddenly a deep bond of common feeling existed between them. . . .*" In their feeling of spiritual homelessness, the O'Neills recognized the common source of their tragedy.

And so Eugene's compulsive building of many mansions became more than the ironic expression of a naïve or hypocritical materialism. In each successive mansion he hoped to discover a true home, even while knowing that he could never feel "it was my home." Even his most stately mansions would always seem temporary and provisional. From Bermuda in 1928 he had written with cautious enthusiasm to a friend: "Next to Peaked Hill [Provincetown] in the old days, I believe this is the most satisfying habitat I've struck. It really has the feeling of home to me, who usually feel in most houses like a Samoan in an igloo."[24] If no worldly habitat could ever be home to O'Neill, "Tao House" came closest.

He lived in "Tao House" for more than six years—longer than he had lived anywhere else. And he left largely for physical reasons. In 1944 the house was sold because of its isolation in wartime and because of his own failing health which required quick access to doctors and to hospitals. When the war ended, he moved back to New York where the final plays which he had written in "Tao House" were produced. And in New York he moved to a hotel, where, busy with the details of the production of *The Iceman*, he was happy for a time.

But the remaining years could bring only tragedy. When a degenerative disease destroys progressively the functioning of a creative mind, frustration and unhappiness are inevitable. After periods of quarreling with Carlotta and of treatment in hospitals, the couple left New York to live in one more mansion. On Marblehead Neck (all the names seem symbolic) where ships sailed by, to and from the Atlantic, they bought and remodeled a house; and they lived there for the remaining years of illness and loneliness. Meanwhile, his disease grew worse. Finally they moved to a hotel in Boston, where doctors could come at a moment's notice. In this hotel, on November 27, 1953, he died.

Eugene O'Neill was born in a Broadway hotel; he died in a Boston hotel. Between his birth and death, he lived in many different houses in many different places. But none could ever become home. The New York hotel in which he had been born was later demolished to make way for modern construction, and he liked to recall that the place of his birth was now only empty air. There seems irony also in the fact that he died in Boston, where so many of his plays had been banned. But he had chosen Boston because it was the medical capital of the modern world (even though no doctors could ever cure his disease). It seems immaterial where or in what hotel or mansion he was born, or lived, or died. No physical place could have been home. For he had built his mansions of the imagination for the dwelling place of the soul.

IX   *"A Great Spirit"*

When Brooks Atkinson wrote O'Neill's obituary, he remembered the quality of the man before that of his work: "A great spirit and our greatest dramatist have left us." And John Gassner echoed the conviction: "He was, above all, a unique personality." Indeed, O'Neill's personal magnetism impressed many men more than his excellence as a dramatist, and his enemies have recognized this personal quality as well as his friends. Francis Fergusson, who disliked most of his plays, nevertheless bore witness that "The man O'Neill is very close to a vast audience."[25] Those who condemned the turbulent passions of O'Neill's early life and criticized the irregularities of his dramatic art nevertheless have recognized his dedication to his work and his total involvement in life. Even though O'Neill's pessimism increased with age, so that he once exclaimed that "the atomic bomb was a wonderful invention because it might annihilate the human race," he never turned his back on the human race. Unlike Robinson Jeffers, who rejected "humanity" for "the tower beyond tragedy," O'Neill always identified himself with humanity in its most tragic forms.

Some have described his personal quality in purely rational terms. Philip Moeller, who directed *Strange Interlude,* recalled: "There was no small meanness about Gene. He had tremendous integrity, was one of the most honest human beings I have ever known." But many have reacted more emotionally: "He was gracious to everyone, and wonderfully alive." And in 1927 Brooks Atkinson had described his first meeting with the playwright: "O'Neill's face is marked with experience. It is not tired. It is vivid, there is something immediately magnetic about his personality. . . . He left me with a glow all afternoon."

Very few famous men have produced this impression of personal sincerity and selflessness, and even fewer men of letters have done so. For most authors have labored so hard to create their literary legends that, like Hemingway, they can justly be accused of cultivating "false hair on the chest." But O'Neill had created no fictional "persona"—the man and the work were one. And other authors have been so tormented by the struggle of creation that their egotism has blinded them to the justice of any criticism. Thomas Wolfe lashed out at the denigrations of Bernard De Voto; but De Voto's attacks on O'Neill were passed in silence. Although naturally troubled by the hostility of destructive criticism, O'Neill was able to accept it objectively. And progressively he achieved that transcendence of personal egotism which is the hallmark of greatness.

The unique feeling of spiritual depth which O'Neill inspired in his lifetime is still suggested by many photographs of the man. The eyes still gaze with a brooding impersonality which seems to focus somewhere within, or beyond their object. Many have tried to describe these eyes—perhaps the Gelbs have best succeeded:

> His eyes, always an astonishment to those meeting him for the first time, illuminated his face. Large, dark, immeasurably deep, set wide apart under heavy brows, they could stare into depths that existed for no one else. When he turned the O'Neill look on someone, he appeared to gaze into that person's soul. But the appraisal was neither critical nor even disconcerting; it was a look of profound and gentle searching, at once penetrating and reassuring. For nothing shocked him. He was interested only in the motive behind the action.[26]

Ultimately the man was one with his plays. And the impression that the author was often one with his audience also persists. An experience of the present writer may illustrate. In 1934 *Days Without End* was being tried out in Boston, and my wife and I had attended a performance. At its end we were walking slowly up the aisle, discussing our perplexity and dissatisfaction with the play's ending, when we became conscious of a man in the aisle seat of the back row observing the audience as it filed past. For a moment the dark eyes rested on us—yet not really on us—rather on our feeling of perplexity, which his eyes seemed to share. Then he rose and hurried out into the wings. Turning to each other in startled surprise, we said: "That was O'Neill."

CHAPTER 2

The Pattern of O'Neill's Tragedies

> Robert. (*Pointing to the horizon—dreamily*)
> Supposing I was to tell you that it's just
> Beauty that's calling me, the beauty of the
> far off and unknown, the mystery and spell of
> the East which lures me in the books I've read,
> the need of the freedom of the great wide
> spaces, the joy of wandering on and on—in
> quest of the secret which is hidden over there,
> beyond the horizon?

THE DREAM of an impossible beauty beyond the horizon always fascinated Eugene O'Neill, and it distinguished all his early writing. Quite simply and directly it inspired the heroes of his early plays, as in *Beyond the Horizon* and *The Fountain*. Then by contrast it emphasized the ugliness of materialistic America, as in *The Great God Brown* and *Marco Millions*. Later, the impossibility of realizing the dream caused the frustration and violence of the major tragedies, *Strange Interlude* and *Mourning Becomes Electra*. But in the center of every drama, no matter how sordid the plot or how common the characters, some scene of idyllic loveliness—some flash of unearthly beauty—appeared.

Although this beauty has always been the subject of lyric poetry, it has been rare in realistic tragedy. For instance, the Celtic imagination of W. B. Yeats has often dwelt upon "The Land of Heart's Desire":

> Where nobody gets old and crafty and wise,
> Where nobody gets old and godly and grave,
> Where beauty has no ebb, decay no flood,
> But joy is wisdom, Time an endless song.

But when the modern dramatist has imagined this land of dream, he has necessarily contrasted it with the world of here and now. And the contrast has emphasized the ugliness of modern reality. This ugliness is the reverse of the medal.

All of O'Neill's power of invention *dramatized this contrast between dream and reality. Sometimes by means of theatrical lighting, as in the visions of *Emperor Jones* and *Marco Millions;* sometimes by means of two planes or of a divided stage, as in *Desire under the Elms* and *Dynamo;* but more often by means of masks, asides, and frank unrealism, he made objective this inner division of the human mind. In his imaginative theater, the dream has been high-lighted and man's subconscious idealizations made articulate to a degree impossible in life. From this artistry a new drama infinitely rich in perspective and depth resulted.

But if the dream of an impossible beauty has given richness to his writing, it has also caused serious distortion. Not that O'Neill's dramatic conception has been confused. And not that the dream has lacked universality: all men have imagined some land of heart's desire, and all Americans especially have hoped to realize it in this "new world." But here is the distortion: although O'Neill's characters have all imagined an ideal beauty, very few have even hoped to realize it. They have dreamed, that is, not of realization but of escape. "Wandering on and on . . . beyond the horizon," they have become lost. And in their confusion their dreams have turned to nightmares.

Because the romantic dreamers of O'Neill's plays have all imagined an impossible perfection, they have necessarily despaired of realizing it. But historically the great dreamers of America have imagined a possible perfection and have sought pragmatically to realize it. Imagining only absolute freedom, O'Neill's romantics have rejected all partial freedoms. And imagining the perfect brotherhood of man, they have rejected actual democracy. In the end, because they have instinctively recognized the impossibility of their romantic absolutes, they have lost faith in the future. And their failure has led them to deny the American faith.

Eugene O'Neill himself, like the heroes of his own dramas, followed this romantic logic to its inevitable end. First, his imagination gloried in the discovery and affirmation of the beauty of his dream. Next, he denounced in ringing words the ugliness of American reality. Then he described the tragic defeat of the romantic dream in actual life. And, at last, the clear recognition of the dream's impossibility led him toward resignation and quiescence.

I *The Romantic Dream*

O'Neill's early plays suggest both the beauty and the impossibility of the romantic dream. From *The Long Voyage Home* to *The Fountain*, his heroes imagine the unreal. With tragic inevitability, they suffer defeat. But, nevertheless, all achieve tragic exaltation by remaining true to their dream. Denying the values of the material world, they transmute defeat into victory. Thus they seem to exemplify "the great truth that there is nothing so precious in our lives as our illusions."[1] "As is true of the great heroes of all tragedies . . . they are destroyed by their virtues."[2]

But all of these early plays describe the romantic dream in such a manner as to suggest that its very impossibility constitutes its beauty. The heroes seem to idealize it *because* it can never be realized. They not only exemplify the truth that nothing is so precious to us as our illusions, but they also imply that our illusions are really more precious than the truth: they praise the will to illusion as if it were man's major virtue. Therefore, the plays, although realistic in dealing with the dream's inevitable defeat, become unrealistic in implying its immeasurable value. For a dream is truly valuable only when it leads toward the realization of some possible ideal.

The impossibility of the romantic dream which inspires these early heroes is sometimes explicitly stated, and always implied. In terms of the sea, the plays describe its two mutually incompatible forms. In the first, the characters dream of perfect peace and security, freed from all the vicissitudes and hardships of the sea. In the second, they dream of romantic adventure and discovery, freed from all the drabness and routine of the farm. One group of dreamers possesses what the other group idealizes, and each imagines the other to be perfectly happy. Both, therefore, seek escape from reality to an impossible ideal.

In his very first play, *Bound East for Cardiff,* O'Neill described the dream of the dying sailor Yank of "a farm with a house of your own with cows and pigs and chickens. . . . It must be great to have a home of your own." And O'Neill repeated this theme throughout his early "Plays of the Sea." And life symbolically became the "Long Voyage Home" toward a security and a peace which could never exist. In *Anna Christie* this impossible ideal of security found its clearest expression and its surest defeat.

But in his first successful play, *Beyond the Horizon*, O'Neill had already described the impossibility of the opposite dream of romantic adventure. And his dream of an escape to "the great wide spaces" of the world was to motivate many of his later plays. Whether seeking "ile" in the Arctic, gold in California, silk in Cathay, or an idyllic love enisled in the South Seas, his heroes were to follow the same rainbow to the same end. Rejecting what security they already possessed, they were all to imagine the romantically impossible and to destroy themselves in their quest for it.

"The beauty of the far off and the unknown, the mystery and spell of the East which lures me in the books I've read" became the actual protagonist of *The Fountain*. In this last and most unrealistic of O'Neill's early plays, "the fountain of youth" (by definition an impossibility) became an actual presence. At first it was described vaguely:

> There is some far country of the East—Cathay, Cipango, who knows—a spot that nature has set apart from men and blessed with peace. It is a sacred grove where all things live in the old harmony they knew before man came . . . and in the center of the grove there is a fountain—beautiful beyond human dreams. . . .

But at the end this fountain appeared visibly: "Oh, Luis, I begin to know eternal youth! I have found my fountain." At the end the "soldier of iron—and dreamer," whose two "selves" had clashed in early life, finally became the perfect dreamer and died gloriously with his dream: "God's will be done in death!"

This romantic philosophy is very beautiful, and O'Neill's early dramas illustrating it described it beautifully. But it is also unreal, and O'Neill's early dramas suffered from this unrealism. In describing the conflict between dream and reality, the dream was always lovely; the reality, always ugly. In response to the challenge: "There is no profit in staking life for dreams," his heroes replied: "There is no profit in anything but that!" It was "all or nothing," and anything less than "all" was nothing.

At first, O'Neill's heroes concentrated on the dream of absolute beauty and found salvation in dying for it. Their dreams remained pure, and their dramas beautiful. Only in the later plays did O'Neill and his characters begin to question the romantic dream and to wonder if its unreality were really as lovely as it seemed. Therefore, the later plays became more realistic but less beautiful.

II   *The American Reality*

In his second group of plays O'Neill turned his attention from the dream of beauty to the ugliness of reality. And by focusing upon the immediate American scene, he achieved greater realism. No longer did he vaguely imagine an impossible ideal. But, in describing present day reality, he did remember the earlier dream and contrast the modern reality with it. Therefore, American "materialism" came to seem excessively ugly. The modern businessman became more than the philistine—he became the very devil's disciple. And the actual practice of American democracy became something to be excoriated. The remembrance of the romantic dream led to the rejection of the actuality.

Like *The Fountain*, *The Hairy Ape* dealt with man's quest for perfection and peace. But where the first had described the pure, religious quest, the second described its social implications. Now "Yank" (the Hairy Ape) dreamed not of abstract beauty but of "belonging." Acutely aware of his social inferiority, he desired an ideal brotherhood of man. And because he could never find this absolutely ideal democracy, he rejected the partial democracy which America could offer. Therefore he could find peace at last only in death, in the arms of a gorilla. But like Juan Ponce de Leon, he did remain true to his dream, and God's will was done in death. Through his tragedy, the negative implications of the dream became more explicit.

Yank—presumably the typical American workingman—did not want a higher standard of living, freedom, or equal rights. Rather, he demanded the dream-remembered harmony of the Garden of Eden. And he was very positive about it all:

. . . Cut out an hour offen de job a day and make me happy! Tree square a day, and cauliflowers in de front yard—ekal rights —a woman and kids—a lousy vote—and I'm all fixed for Jesus, huh? Aw, hell! What does dat get yuh? Dis ting's in your inside. . . .

Our "lousy" American democracy was not for him, because he envisioned an ideal democracy. For this impossible unreality he denied both the democratic actual and also the democratic possible. With present American reality, he rejected future American possibility. Both were "materialistic" and ugly.

The Great God Brown magnified this American dualism of the materialistic and the romantic to universal proportions. William A. Brown—like his contemporary American, George F. Babbitt—became the "god" of our materialism. But in rejecting this false American "god," O'Neill's hero again rejected American democracy: Dion turned away from "the rabble" because "he hated to share with them fountain, flame and fruit." That is, his romantic idealism became wholly negative. Like other Americans, he even began to worship the devil because God would not grant him his absolute ideal: "When Pan was forbidden the light and warmth of the sun he grew sensitive and self-conscious and proud and revengeful—and became Prince of Darkness." And so Dion the romantic dreamer turned against the American world in which he lived.

In *Marco Millions,* O'Neill contrasted the materialism of the workaday world more universally with the romantic "mystery and spell of the East." The modern Marco—alias George F. Babbitt, alias the Great God Brown—became the arch-enemy of all things beautiful and spiritual—truly an instrument of evil. And at the end the great Kaan's voice proclaimed "with pitying scorn: 'The Word became their flesh, they say. Now all is flesh! And can their flesh become the Word again?'"

This question goes to the heart of O'Neill's thought and work. And the answer—which had lain implicit in his earlier plays— became increasingly explicit in his later ones: Man cannot achieve salvation until he renounces all worldly materialism, accepts the defeat which his dream implies, and returns to spiritual faith. In striving for practical goods, man denies the ideal Good. In seeking to improve the Flesh, he forgets the

[70]

Word. Therefore, according to O'Neill, modern man should renounce all belief in materialistic progress and strive only for ideal perfection.

This has always been the logic of absolutism. The ideal world is good, and man instinctively worships it. The material world is bad, but man is unable to perfect it. Therefore, man should renounce the material for the absolute ideal. The early dramas had described the ideal perfection. The later ones denounced the material imperfection. It remained for the major dramas to portray the inner conflict of good and evil leading to the great renunciation.

III *The Human Tragedy*

Lazarus Laughed, Strange Interlude, and *Mourning Becomes Electra* form a kind of trilogy. Not only are they among O'Neill's most successful dramas, but, on different levels of action, they carry forward his romantic logic to its inevitable conclusion. Together, they describe the human tragedy of modern man, in contrast to "The Divine Comedy" of earlier times. In the first, Lazarus realizes the paradisaic beauty of an impossible ideal. In the second, Nina Leeds struggles through a purgatorial compromise between the ideal and the actual. Finally, Lavinia Mannon recognizes the impossibility of achieving the ideal and symbolically accepts damnation for man's materialism. Written in this order and moving down these steps of logic, these three dramas describe the tragedy of man who envisions the perfect, struggles vainly to achieve it, and finally accepts inevitable defeat.

Lazarus Laughed is the most ideal of all O'Neill's works. It was his own favorite.[3] It is one of the finest dramas of pure mysticism in the language. Yet it has never been produced professionally. Among the major works of America's first dramatist, it alone has never become popular. Its beauty remains strangely remote. If the reason for this lies partly in the unpopularity of all mysticism, it also lies in the peculiarly absolute quality of O'Neill's mysticism.

This modern Lazarus becomes the archetype of all O'Neill's unworldly dreamers. Like the hero of *Beyond the Horizon,* he had always been "impractical" and a "failure in life." Like the hero of *The Fountain,* he had been "born a dreamer," who can realize his ideal only in death. But now *Lazarus Laughed* actually begins where *The Fountain* ended—with the death of its hero. The plot follows the life of Lazarus *after* his resurrection from the grave. In human terms, it seeks to describe the "practical effect" of "the fountain of youth" upon the divine hero and upon his human followers.

The greatness of this drama is that it translates the dream of divine perfection into human terms. Lazarus himself incarnates the perfection, and the various imperfect human beings who come under his influence illustrate various aspects of it. The psychological reactions of these people are convincing, and their physical reactions seem natural, for the most part. The conflict between Roman materialism and Christian idealism is imaginatively realized in both words and acts. Lazarus truly speaks and lives like one who has overcome the human fear of pain and death and has now learned to live life affirmatively—freed from the negative dread of losing his own.

But the weakness of *Lazarus Laughed* is that this absolutely perfect hero fails to move us. His sorrows and sufferings leave us cold because, if he does not feel pain and fear, neither do we feel them for him. Only the natural reactions of other men toward him truly move us—and, paradoxically, the vestiges of human weakness which this all-too-perfect Lazarus sometimes betrays. When he stretches out his hand to prevent his wife, Miriam, from eating the poisoned peach which the Romans offer her, we feel the thrill of recognition. But, when he himself dies without apparent emotion, we remain unmoved. The tragedy of absolute perfection is not tragic.

And if it be objected that Lazarus merely realizes the ideal of Jesus: "Be ye therefore perfect even as your Father which is in heaven is perfect," the answer is that no man can possibly realize such absolute perfection. Even Jesus cried out in despair on the cross: "My God, why hast Thou forsaken me?" And his human cry has echoed down the ages. But O'Neill's mystical Lazarus does dramatically realize the impossible. And O'Neill, in his other plays, either damns his human protagonists for not also realizing the impossible, or praises them for rejecting the possible in favor of their dream of an impossible perfection— only the impossible is truly good.

Strange Interlude, on the other hand, describes the all-too-human compromises of Nina Leeds in her attempt to realize the ideal life which the death of her fiancé, Gordon Shaw, has denied her. Through subterfuge and deception she moves toward the fulfillment of her human desires. Where *Lazarus Laughed* dramatized perfection, *Strange Interlude* dramatizes imperfection.

But unlike *Lazarus Laughed*, which was ideally perfect, *Strange Interlude* proved deeply moving. In spite of its irregularity and its extreme length, it was translated more often than any of O'Neill's other plays.[4] In its characters human audiences recognized themselves and their own failures to realize their own ideals. This dramatization of the sources of human imperfection seemed more significant than the dramatization of superhuman perfection.

The plot of *Strange Interlude* is contrived to dramatize the conflicts and compromises of imperfect man. Because Nina's ideal love cannot be realized, her actual love must be divided among three different men: husband, lover, and father. And the motives underlying these imperfect types of love are made more clear by means of subconscious thoughts spoken by the characters. No early drama of O'Neill's equals this in subtlety of characterization or sharpness of conflict. Man's sinful compromises with his ideal are fully realized in terms of character and action.

Yet the plot of *Strange Interlude* is artificially contrived to make the normal achievement of true love impossible and to make this weak compromise inevitable. Not only is the ideal lover killed before the action begins, but the substitute husband is arbitrarily declared insane. Thus the ideal, which might at least have been partially realized, is denied. And this device of insanity is truly arbitrary and romantic, resembling *Jane Eyre* and the old Gothic novels rather than modern realistic fiction. It merely declares in dramatic terms the impossibility of the realization of human dreams.

Thus *Strange Interlude* pointed to the conclusion toward which O'Neill's thought had steadily been moving. Because man's dream is impossible and because man by nature is materialistic and sinful, his very attempt to realize his dream in this world must lead him into the evil which he seeks to escape. The very nature of his dream dooms him: "'Romantic imagination! It has ruined more lives than all the diseases! Other diseases, I should say! It's a form of insanity!'" That same romantic dream of human perfection, which at first seemed so beautiful, has actually become the source of all evil.

Mourning Becomes Electra carried this logic to its bitter conclusion and ended O'Neill's long quest of "the secret hidden beyond the horizon." And because the logic of romantic tragedy has always been perfectly negative, this drama attained a kind of diabolical perfection. Where *Lazarus Laughed* described an impossible divine perfection and *Strange Interlude* described a typically human imperfection, *Mourning Becomes Electra* described an almost perfect human depravity. It reached a dead end of denial.

The exact plotting of this modern Electra story and the subtle psychology by which the old myth is modernized are perhaps less important than the romantic theme of "the Blessed Isles," which motivates it. Against a somber background of Yankee "materialism," the characters describe their "dream" of peace in some ideal island of the South Seas. First Adam Brant, who has actually been there, tells Lavinia of these isles. Then Orin Mannon describes his dreams of them, suggested by reading Melville's *Typee*: "I read it and reread it until finally those Islands came to mean everything that wasn't war, everything that was peace and warmth and security. I used to dream I was there . . . —the most beautiful island in the world—as beautiful as you, Mother!"

Then on board the clipper ship, in the central scene of the play, Brant and Christine Mannon plan their actual escape to "the Blessed Isles—Maybe we can still find happiness and forget!" But the avenging furies strike, and the family destroys itself until only Lavinia is left. But she raises the play to greatness by her denial of the romantic dream which has fooled all the others. Her final words seem both literal and symbolic: "'Tell Hannah to throw out all the flowers.'" The old dream of ideal beauty has been discarded.

IV *A Letter from O'Neill*

Logically, this negation should be the end: if perfection is impossible and if reality is an ugly truth that must grimly be endured, then "the rest is silence." And for fifteen years after writing *Mourning Becomes Electra,* O'Neill kept comparatively silent. Once, in *Dynamo,* he retold the tragedy of American materialism. Twice he sought to salvage some comfort from despair: *Ah, Wilderness!* reaffirmed the beauty of the romantic dream, and *Days Without End* preached the value of an immaterial faith. But he refused from 1934 to 1946 to allow the publication or production of any new play.

This refusal may have been artistic caution. But more probably his long silence was caused by his failure to find a way out of the alley into which his logic had led. If man's dream of perfection is impossible and if worldly compromise is ignoble and materialistic, then man is doomed to despair in this world. The alternatives to the old American ideal of progress were the romantic dream of beauty, the romantic reaction of despair, and the other-worldly religion of comfort. O'Neill had explored the beauty beyond the horizon and the wasteland of despair. But he had not found "the secret hidden over there," nor did it seem in 1945, that he had reconciled himself to the impossibility of finding it.

But from 1939 to 1943 he had been writing the final tragedies which many now believe to be his greatest. And in 1945 he wrote a long letter commenting on my preceding critique of his plays, which had just been published.[5] In this letter he fully approved the description of his earlier dramas as romantic, but he also affirmed his belief in the superiority of his final dramas, as yet unpublished.

March 24th 1945

My dear Mr. Carpenter:

I am extremely grateful for your courtesy in sending me a copy of your "The Romantic Tragedy of Eugene O'Neill." I have read it with the greatest pleasure and satisfaction and I find it a sound piece of critical interpretation. Of course, there is this and that to which I take exception, but what of it. The main thing is that I feel so keenly that you really hit what is below the surface. . . .

I am particularly grateful for the high place you give "Lazarus Laughed." I do not rate it as my best now. "Mourning Becomes Electra" is—of all the old plays. "Long Day's Journey into Night" written in '40 - '41 is the best of all, I now think. And "The Iceman Cometh" written in '39 - '40 is surely one of the top flight. So I think is "A Moon for the Misbegotten" written in

'41. [*sic*] As for the Cycle of nine plays, ("A Tale of Possessors
Self-Dispossessed"), covering a period from 1775-1932, I put
that on the shelf in 1939, with three of the plays in first draft
and one finished. For the past two years I've done nothing at
all. My health has had me down, as has been the case more or
less frequently since my crack-up in '36 - '37—operation, months
in hospital, etc. . . .

   Again, much gratitude for your article. You will find in "The
Iceman Cometh," which will be the first to be produced when I
decide to produce, much that will agree with your last sentence—
and much that won't!

Very sincerely,
(signed) Eugene O'Neill

This letter is interesting for several reasons. First, O'Neill
heartily accepted the description of his early dramas as
"romantic," and he did not object to the explicit criticism of
their anti-pragmatic bias. His own interpretation of "American
reality" had always been negative, and it remained so. The
historic American philosophy, which has defined the ideal in
terms of the pragmatically possible, seemed to him merely
materialistic. Therefore his own American "heroes," "the great
god Brown" and "Marco Millions," had merely denied all
American idealisms. And this negative logic of romantic absolutism perhaps led him to abandon his projected Cycle of nine
plays dealing with the history of an American family ("A Tale
of Possessors Self-Dispossessed"). Even the single drama which
he salvaged from the Cycle ("A Touch of the Poet") seemed to
him not worth considering among "my best."

But three of his late dramas, which did not deal with American
history (except in personal terms), seemed to him "top flight."
And *Long Day's Journey* was "the best of all." With this
opinion of the author, modern critical judgment, from 1946 to
the present, has enthusiastically agreed. The three plays, which
he wrote after his "crackup" and between the frequent visits to
the hospital which signaled the onset of that tragic nervous
disorder which finally caused his death, include two of his
greatest. Not the five years of good health which followed the
writing of *Mourning Becomes Electra,* therefore, but the years
of increasingly ill health which followed them produced his

greatest dramas. There can be no physical explanation for this fact. His final dramas merely transcended the romantic logic which had governed his earlier work; they took off into a new dimension.

O'Neill himself hinted obliquely at this new logic: "You will find in *The Iceman Cometh*," he wrote, "much that will agree with your last sentence—and much that won't!" (The "last sentence" had complained: "He has not yet found 'the secret hidden over there,' nor has he fully reconciled himself to the impossibility of finding it.") *The Iceman* now described dramatically the impossibility of man's "pipe-dreams" of finding the secret of life; and, in the process of this dramatic description, the play suggested the author's reconciliation with this tragic impossibility. It is this final reconciliation, perhaps, which enabled O'Neill to transcend the earlier tragedies of his own dramatic creation and to achieve that perfect objectivity which only the greatest writers have ever achieved.

V   *Transcendence*

In his final dramas, O'Neill no longer celebrated the romantic dreams of his characters, nor condemned their selfish materialism, nor even participated emotionally in their human tragedies. Rather, he transcended both the actions and the passions which he described, so that his characters seemed to live out their tragedies without help or hindrance of author. The final dramas ceased to be romantic and became "transcendental."

But the author's transcendence of his material and his achievement of objectivity toward it did not diminish the earthy realism or the emotional intensity of the tragedies—rather, the reverse. These final dramas actually seem more real—and they actually are more autobiographical—than the early ones. Their "transcendence" lies not in the subject matter but in the author's disinvolvement from it. By his own account, O'Neill wrote *Long Day's Journey* "with deep pity and understanding and forgiveness for *all* the four haunted Tyrones." In these dramas he transcended both his own earlier self and the earlier romantic tragedy that he had produced.

In all the earlier dramas, he had identified himself emotionally with one of his characters, and he had condemned others. In *The Great God Brown*, for instance, he obviously sympathized with Dion Anthony, the sensitive dreamer, rather than with Billy Brown, the unfeeling materialist. In *Desire Under the Elms* (which has been described as an "unconscious autobiographical drama"), he identified with the young Eben Cabot's opposition to his unfeeling father, Ephraim. And in *Marco Millions*, his identification with "the great Kaan" (a dramatic incarnation of "the mystery and spell of the East which lures me in the books I've read") became complete, as did his condemnation of the materialistic Marco. But in the later plays, O'Neill kept himself aloof. In *The Iceman*, he no longer identified with the sensitive philosopher, Larry, who suffered from "the wrong kind of pity." And in *Long Day's Journey*, he achieved objectivity even toward his autobiographical self.

The true subject of these final dramas—as of all the earlier ones—is still the romantic dream of beauty, and "the secret which is hidden over there, beyond the horizon." But whereas the earlier plays had celebrated this dream and whereas *Strange Interlude* and *Mourning Becomes Electra* had denounced the "disease" of the romantic imagination, the final dramas neither celebrate nor denounce. Just as the later O'Neill held himself aloof from his heroes, and neither sympathized with nor criticized them, so he described their "pipe-dreams" with equal objectivity. Both the petty self-deceptions of the drunken denizens of Harry Hope's saloon and the major self-delusion of Hickey, the salesman of salvation, seem to exist "beyond good and evil." But, unlike the early imaginings of the early dramas, they no longer suggest a Nietzschean immoralism. The later plays do not deny the reality of good and evil—they transcend it.

This final transcendence finds its most perfect expression in O'Neill's most perfect play. *Long Day's Journey Into Night* dramatizes the fundamental fact of human evil but never denounces it. The mother's progressive retreat from reality into the ultimate "pipe-dream" of opium addiction is never described as evil. But its causes in the actions of the father and of society, and its effects upon the sufferings of the father and of his sons, are dramatized with perfect objectivity. The tangled web of self-deception which leads to the final tragedy is laid bare. But the final result is neither sentimental pity, nor moral condemnation, but perfect understanding: *"Tout comprendre, c'est tout pardonner."*

The "transcendental" tragedy of the later O'Neill achieves a goal much like that of the Oriental religion and philosophy which "lured" O'Neill throughout his life, and which found final expression in "Tao House." In the final tragedies, the veil of Maya seems to be torn aside and all the illusions of human life laid bare. Romantic dreams are exposed as the delusions they are. And yet, unlike O'Neill's earlier dramas and unlike all the romantic literature of the modern Occident, these dreams are no longer seen as beautiful, nor are they seen as evil. Rather, they are recognized as the very substance of human life. As Larry remarks in *The Iceman*: "The lie of a pipe dream is what gives life to the whole misbegotten mad lot of us, drunk or sober." The veil of Maya is the substance of life itself.

But the goal of life, then, is the recognition that all man's dreams and romantic imaginings are, indeed, illusions. When man accepts the fact that he can never find "the secret hidden over there" and reconciles himself to the impossibility of finding it, he may realize perfect peace. When the veil of Maya is torn aside, he may achieve an approximation of Nirvana. This modern philosophy of tragedy, which sees man's life as necessarily doomed to defeat, but also suggests that man's recognition of the necessity of defeat may constitute a kind of victory, arrives at much the same goal as the most important religions of the Orient. But with one significant difference.

Tragedy offers the means of distancing and of rendering acceptable man's recognition of the necessary defeat of his dreams. In the "temple" of the tragic theater, the artistic ritual of man's doom is acted out before an actual audience. And this formal tragedy, viewed objectively, can then be recognized as symbolic reality. By dramatizing man's romantic dreams and acting out their inevitable defeat, O'Neill was able to remove his tragedy from the realm of realistic description to that of transcendent art. Thus distanced, his tragic audience could contemplate with equanimity the illusory nature of their dreams and desires. And the Oriental Nirvana, or the stilling of human desires, could then become the transcendence of these desires and the recognition of their illusory nature.

VI *The Final Tragedies*

The final tragedies which O'Neill wrote in his declining years
—*The Iceman Cometh, Long Day's Journey Into Night,* and
A Moon for the Misbegotten—also form a kind of trilogy. But,
unlike the earlier "trilogy" of *Lazarus Laughed, Strange Interlude,* and *Mourning Becomes Electra,* which described in
descending order man's fall from a paradisaic ideal through a
purgatorial compromise to a hell of denial and despair, this
final trilogy describes the soul's ascent from the depths. *The
Iceman* dramatizes the coming of "death," but it suggests that
despair may be transcended by the understanding of man's
romantic illusions. *Long Day's Journey* describes the purgatorial
life of the Tyrone family, who hope that the mother may conquer
her dope-addiction but who learn finally to understand the
reasons for it. And *A Moon* suggests the final peace that results
from a strange kind of love stripped of all romantic illusions.

This final trilogy may also be described in terms of the
symbolic time in which the actions occur. *The Iceman* develops
in the half-light of a dim, alcoholic world, and it ends,
symbolically, after midnight: "around 1:30 A.M." *Long Day's
Journey* describes the more normal events of daily life, but
it also ends after midnight, having explored the dark night of
the human soul. Finally, most of the action of *A Moon* takes
place by moonlight, but the last act ends, symbolically, at
daybreak. O'Neill's final tragedy might have been named "Long
Night's Vigil for the Dawn." The spiritual death which "the
iceman" symbolizes has often been emphasized by the critics,
and the dark night in which the "long day's journey" ends is
emphasized by the title; but O'Neill's own dramatic career ended
with this symbolic sunrise. Nevertheless, he greeted this new day
sardonically and without illusions at the end of *A Moon*; for
Hogan asks Josie: "Are you going to moon at the sunrise forever?"

If these final tragedies form a sort of trilogy and if their
action advances from twilight through night to sunrise, these
dramas are as unlike the traditional *Inferno, Purgatorio,* and
Paradiso as can be imagined. Each O'Neill play contains a
mixture of rowdy comedy with grim tragedy, and the mood of
each remains ironically ambivalent. If *The Iceman* describes a
kind of human hell, in whose lower depths men find their wills

paralyzed and their emotions frozen, as Dante's Satan was frozen in the depths of the *Inferno*, it also describes a drunken comradeship in which men can at last "belong." If *Long Day's Journey* describes the purgatorial sufferings of the auto-biographical hero, it also recalls the exaltation of his mystical experiences at sea, and it suggests his future recovery and final victory. And conversely, if *A Moon* ends without actual hope and within the shadow of the death of James Tyrone, it still brings the promise of peace and a sort of salvation.

Throughout his career, O'Neill's dramatic thought followed a fairly clear, consistent course. First, he celebrated the romantic dream, and his heroes achieved exaltation by means of it. Next, he described the tragedy of an American materialism divorced from all dreams. Then, with Lazarus, he imagined perfection. But progressively he realized the distortions and delusions inherent in the romantic imagination of man. Having lost faith in the dream, he projected a cycle of tragedies to describe the decline of an American family through history. But, having lost faith, he found that he could no longer create successfully. Finally, by facing down the delusions of his own autobiographical past, he transcended his despair. Within these actual delusions—within the drunken fellowship of his beachcomber days, the natural violence of his life at sea, and the twisted relationships of his own family—he found the possibility of transcendence. But this possibility no longer lay in a romantic Beauty beyond the horizon. It lay, rather, in Josie Hogan's pigsty.

CHAPTER 3

The Early Plays: Romance

I   S. S. Glencairn

O'NEILL WRITES: *"There is silence for a second or so, broken only by the haunted, saddened voice of that brooding music, faint and far-off, like the mood of the moonlight made audible."* This typically poetic stage direction, which ends *The Moon of the Caribbees,* illustrates both the quality of O'Neill's dramatic imagination, the nature of his theatrical technique, and the essential subject matter of all his tragedies. From the beginning to the end of his career, he emphasized that "touch of the poet" which he believed to be the most important (and the most overlooked) element, both of his own nature and of his writing. Throughout his career, he supplied occasional stage directions to suggest the spirit of the theatrical effects which he desired, rather than the details of their implementation. And all his plays dramatized the subject matter of romance: from *The Moon of the Caribbees* to *A Moon for the Misbegotten,* some moon—or some of the delusions which that orb traditionally begets—dominated his tragedies.

The chief difference between his early plays and his later ones lies in the nature of the romance described and in the technique by which it is dramatized. His early plays deal with physical moonlight and pure romance, and they dramatize these simply and directly. But the later plays deal with those psychological illusions which the moon has traditionally induced, and they dramatize these more indirectly. In the early plays, romance finds itself both dramatized and celebrated. But the later plays describe romance much more ironically. Perhaps for this reason, the early plays have inspired the best of the many motion pictures to be based on O'Neill's work—including two of the best pictures which Hollywood has produced.

Although *The Moon of the Caribbees* was not the first of O'Neill's plays about the sea, it was placed first when the four *S. S. Glencairn* plays were produced as a unit in 1924 (with O'Neill's blessing), and when they were collected for publication in 1926. And its "mood of the moonlight made audible" naturally introduces the theme of all of them. Followed by *Bound East for Cardiff*, *The Long Voyage Home*, and *In the Zone*, this group has been frequently revived. And in 1940 these plays were adapted by Hollywood for the picture *The Long Voyage Home.*

The physical background of the sea, given in rich and concrete detail by O'Neill's introductory stage directions, also produced a stunning pictorial setting for the motion picture: *"On the left two of the derrick booms of the foremast jut out at an angle of forty-five degrees, black against the sky. In the rear the dark outline of the port bulwark is sharply defined against a distant strip of coral beach white in the moonlight. . . ."* Photographic realism combines with poetic evocation to suggest that background of sensuous and imaginative reality against which all of his plays have acted themselves out—whether on the stage, on the screen, or in the reader's imagination.

The action of *The Moon of the Caribbees* is unimportant. A group of sailors on deck are passing the time talking and quarreling, while awaiting the arrival of smuggled rum and women. These arrive; the talking and the quarreling increase in volume; a fight breaks out; a man is knifed; the officers intervene; and the rum and women are sent away. The routine of boredom has been broken for a moment, but the romance ends; only the moonlight and the haunted echo of distant music remain.

But, if the action is unimportant, the characterization of the seamen who live on the *S. S. Glencairn* is memorable. Like the sailors who inhabit the ships of Melville's imaginary voyages, they are chosen to represent the nations of the world; but they are more individualized, and are drawn recognizably from life: many have been identified with actual seamen with whom O'Neill sailed the seas, or with whom he drank at "Jimmy the Priest's" and "The Hell Hole." Although "Yank" was later to

become symbolic when he went on shore in *The Hairy Ape* he
remained on the S. S. *Glencairn* wholly an individual.

First to speak in ONeill's first play (and last to speak in his
last) is the Irishman (here "Driscoll"), strong, loyal, humorous,
and not too bright. With him is "Yank," more enterprising, and
honest; when the women are to be paid off, he sees to it that they
are not cheated. Most interesting is "Smitty," a lost soul, seemingly uninterested in women, somewhat outside the group, and
therefore a natural focus for distrust and abuse. Although a
more "modern" dramatist might have made him a psycho-sexual
aberrant, he remains simply the unhappy outsider. "Cocky," the
compulsive boaster; "Olson," the dumb "square-'ead," and "Ivan,"
the "rooshin," complete the main group. But whatever their
nationality or nature, and however primitive or typical their
characters, they speak with the breath of life; and they act with
a convincing reality which has impressed critics and audiences
from the beginning. As Alexander Woollcott wrote of a later
play, O'Neill always seemed to possess "the surplus creative
energy which enables him, after the essential structure of the
play has been attended to, to people it with original and distinctive characters, brought into the theatre with the breath of life
in them."[1]

O'Neill considered *The Moon of the Caribbees* the best of
his one-act plays. He valued it most because it broke with the
tradition of the commercial theater by dispensing with formal
action in order to develop more effectively mood, emotion, and
character. From the beginning, these qualities have been the
hallmarks of his best plays.

Second of the *Glencairn* plays, but first to be written, and the
first of all to be produced, is *Bound East for Cardiff*. Later,
O'Neill commented on it to a critic: "Very important from my
point of view. In it can be seen, or felt, the germ of the spirit,
life-attitude, etc., of all my more important future work.[2] This
play resembles *The Moon* in that its action is unimportant. But it
introduces what are to be the central themes and symbols of
all the later plays: death, religion, and the eternal "fog" which
blinds men in their quest for truth. The play takes place "on a
foggy night midway on the voyage between New York and
Cardiff." It describes with simple realism the death of "Yank"
from injuries incurred in the line of duty. And it centers upon

his deep anxiety in meeting death (he had once killed a man in a fight), and his feeling of frustration at never having realized his dream of peace and security.

"Dream, Drunkenness, and Death"[3] have been described as the subject matter of O'Neill's dramaturgy, and as the key to all his plays. Drunkenness was the theme of *The Moon*; Dream and Death are central in *Bound East for Cardiff*, the first and perhaps the best of the early plays. And these themes were repeated again in *Long Day's Journey Into Night*, the last and the best. Is O'Neill's "spirit and life-attitude" morbid, pessimistic, and depressing, in these plays—as has often been argued? The question is crucial; and in *Bound East*, a simple play, the answer is implicit, but clear.

This first play begins—as do all the last plays—with pure comedy: Cocky is boasting of his love affair with "the queen of the cannibal isles," and Driscoll is ridiculing his boast. But in the background Yank is lying broken in his bunk. The other seamen go out to take their watch, but Driscoll remains alone with Yank and his tragedy. Yet the important thing about this play—as about the final tragedies also—is the warmth and sincerity of the friendship of two defeated and disillusioned men. As they talk of their memories, the depth of their feeling and the rich comradeship of their life together outweigh their defeat and Yank's fear of death. Yank's greatest fear is: "For God's sake don't leave me alone!" And even "The Mate" of the ship sympathizes and excuses Driscoll from his watch so that he may remain with his dying friend. In this first play, Yank and Driscoll wholly "belong." Dream, Drunkenness and Death do not depress; they lead to a victory over death.

At the end of the play, Driscoll is kneeling beside the dead Yank:

> Cocky. (*enters, oilskins and sou'wester glistening with drops of water*) The fog's lifted. (*Cocky sees Driscoll and stands staring at him with open mouth. Driscoll makes the sign of the cross again*)
>
> Cocky. (*mockingly*) Sayin' 'is prayers! (*He catches sight of the still figure in the bunk and an expression of awed understanding comes over his face . . .*)
>
> Cocky. (*in a hushed whisper*) Gawd blimey!

At the end of this first play the religious emotion of awed understanding, beyond the fog of delusion, finds fulfillment. The play realizes dramatically the emotional experience of the brotherhood of man in the face of death. And the traditional religion symbolized by the sign of the cross is equated with the primitive awe expressed by the final imprecation of "Gawd blimey!"

The third play of the sea, *The Long Voyage Home,* is perhaps the least interesting. With honest realism it tells how a crewman discharged from the *Glencairn* is shanghaied for service on a worse ship. The sober Olson, "with round, childish blue eyes," meets a fate worse than that of his drunken companions. And now conscious evil, in the person of "Fat Joe," the proprietor of "a low dive on the London waterfront," does him in. But, in O'Neill's best plays, it is the unconscious evil and the weakness of human nature that cause tragedy.

The last of the *Glencairn* plays has always been the most popular. *In the Zone* was appreciated by its first reviewers, was incorporated in the routine of a vaudeville company, brought its author his first large royalties, formed the climax of the motion picture, "The Long Voyage Home," and supplies the last act of the S. S. *Glencairn.* But O'Neill himself never liked it; he felt that *"The Moon* works with truth, . . . while *In the Zone* substitutes theatrical sentimentalism." This play is something of a "tear-jerker." Where the earlier plays dramatized objectively the romance and the tragedy of men who go to sea, this dramatized pathos.

"Smitty," the outsider among the crew, is now suspected by his mates of being a German spy (it is wartime and the setting is in a submarine zone) because he guards a black, metal box under his bunk. They bind him and seize the box but they find only old love letters telling why his former love rejected him. Smitty weeps with humiliation: *"his shoulders continue to heave spasmodically."* But his mates also suffer: *"there is a moment of silence, in which each man is in agony with the hopelessness of finding a word he can say."* The exaggeration of Smitty's emotion and the exaggerated language of the love letters which his shipmates read aloud in his presence emphasize the sentimentalism. But the mute hopelessness of his mates, when they recognize the enormity of their mistake, helps to right the balance. *S. S. Glencairn,* like *Long Day's Journey,* ends with genuine tragic recognition.

II Beyond the Horizon

Beyond the Horizon was O'Neill's first full-length play to be produced and to achieve success. Earlier he had written unsuccessful long plays, but now for the first time, the opportunity for development of plot and character which the longer form offered coincided with the development of his own dramatic ideas. In the episodic *S. S. Glencairn* his characters had faced static situations. It is true that *In The Zone* helped to explain why "Smitty" had seemed so uninterested in women in the earlier *The Moon of the Caribbees.* But for the most part, the characters had merely remembered, subjectively, their past lives. Olson, for instance, had idealized the happiness he might have achieved *if* he had stayed home on the family farm. Now, O'Neill reported, "I thought, 'What if he had stayed on the farm, with his instincts? What would have happened?'" Answering his own question, he developed the story of a born wanderer who had denied "his instincts" and had "stayed on the farm."

Beyond the Horizon describes the tragic deterioration of Robert Mayo, his brother Andrew, and the woman they both love. Robert has always dreamed of going away to sea "beyond the horizon," but he changes his plans when Ruth tells him that she really loves him, and not his practical brother. When they marry, the disappointed Andrew runs away to sea. In the second act, the farm has deteriorated under the impractical management of Robert, and his wife Ruth, who has recognized her mistake in marrying him, has grown to hate him. Robert, who also has become embittered, now tells his visiting brother: "I've given up dreaming." In the final act Robert has contracted tuberculosis, and the successful Andrew returns too late to help him. Finally, the dying Robert struggles to the top of a hill, where he can again see the horizon. There he proclaims: "You mustn't feel sorry for me. Don't you see I'm happy at last——free——free! freed from the farm——free to wander on and on——eternally!"

The structure of the play emphasizes the conflict of the two opposing ideals of adventure and security; of the two brothers

who embody them; and—most important—of the two ideals
within the minds of the two brothers. Each act consists of two
scenes: one, on the top of a hill looking toward the horizon;
the other, in the sitting room of a farmhouse. In the first act,
Robert, on the hill top, proclaims his dream of "the beauty of the
far off and the unknown"; then he descends to the farmhouse to
announce that he is marrying Ruth and remaining on the farm.
In the second act, Robert and Ruth act out their frustrations in
the farmhouse; then on the hill top Andrew tells Robert about
his disillusioning adventures in the "East you used to rave about."
In the final act Robert learns in the farmhouse of the hopelessness of his disease, but he escapes to the hill to die with his
dream. The very neatness of this pattern has sometimes disturbed
the critics, and the frequent changes of scene which it involves
have inconvenienced the producers.

The subtlety and complexity of the play derive from the
modulations of this pattern which the action develops and from
the conflicts within the minds of the brothers which it describes.
On the surface, Robert is the pure dreamer, defeated by
practical problems; Andrew, the gross materialist, unable to
dream. But actually Robert is defeated by the delusive quality
of his own dreams. When he abandons his dream of the sea for
marriage and security on the farm, he rationalizes: "you see
I've found——a bigger dream." But actually he has substituted
a deluded dream of "love" for his true dream (true to his
instinctive nature, that is) of adventure. And (Andrew, in turn,
tries to apply his business-like practicality to life at sea, but he
fails partially because he too is infected by a false dream of easy
profits.) Both their failures are therefore caused—not by the
impracticality of the one, and the materialism of the other—but
by the failure of each to recognize his true nature.

The weakness of the play lies in the fact that the character
of Robert Mayo, the nature of his romantic dream of a beauty
beyond the horizon, and—most of all—the attitude of the author
toward this dream seem to vacillate. In the first act, Robert
proclaims his dream eloquently; in the second, he renounces it
flatly; in the final act, he proclaims: "(*Exultingly*) 'All our suffering has been a test through which we had to pass to prove our-
selves worthy of a finer realization.'"——But the question remains: does he really believe this? Is he merely deluding himself?

Is his feeling of having achieved "freedom" in the face of death genuine? That is, has Robert Mayo achieved the self-recognition of the true tragic hero? It seems rather that he protests too much. Yet O'Neill's other plays of this period seem to affirm both the beauty and the truth of this romantic dream.

Paradoxically, *Beyond the Horizon* concludes, and achieves its finest tragic effect, not with Robert Mayo's proclamation of freedom in death, but with Ruth Mayo's acceptance of defeat. At the end Andrew tries to comfort himself: "I——you——we've both made a mess of things! We must try to help each other—— and——in time——we'll come to know what's right——(*Desperately*) And perhaps we——." But Ruth *"remains silent, gazing at him dully with the sad humility of exhaustion, her mind already sinking back into that spent calm beyond the further troubling of any hope."*

III   The Emperor Jones

The Emperor Jones, in every way extraordinary, is "the play that made O'Neill famous." From its first reading by the Provincetown Players, it aroused tremendous enthusiasm. Their experimental production of it started such an "avalanche of applause" that a Broadway producer soon took over. The performance by Charles Gilpin in the title role marked the first major success by a Negro actor on the American stage; later performances by Paul Robeson were anticlimactic. Theatrical critics of the time agreed in praising the play, and most modern critics have repeated the praise. It enjoyed popular success, with a continuous run of 204 performances. In 1933, made into an opera, it was produced in New York by the Metropolitan Company. In foreign countries it has proved equally popular. Moreover, its concentration and brevity have made it attractive to readers and anthologists alike. Wherever modern drama is produced or read, it is familiar.

The limitations of this drama are those inherent in its form and nature. It is half the normal length; and, even in its first production, it had to be pieced out with a one-act comedy. Its quality of intense concentration is reflected in the original physical manuscript, which O'Neill wrote in a tiny, penciled script on both sides of three sheets of typewriting paper. Its concentration of form made necessary the exclusion of major characters other than the hero and also of the realistic detail and development characteristic of the usual play. Negative criticism has called it a "tour-de-force" and has complained of its "melodramatic" nature. Yet it is a "tour-de-force" only in that it is unique, and it is "melodramatic" only in that it shares the emotional primitivism of many operatic stories. On its own terms and within its own limitations, it is a drama completely realized and perfectly motivated.

The Emperor Jones is unique among O'Neill's plays, also, for its lack of any autobiographical background. It was created *de novo* from a mixture of folk tale and imagination, without apparent reference to the psychological problems of the author, or to the actual people he had known; and it recalls only his brief experience in the jungles of Honduras. Its tragedy is the product, not of O'Neill's private experience, but of the universal experience of the race as reflected by his creative imagination.

The story is that of an ex-Pullman porter, Brutus Jones, who has made himself "emperor" of a West Indian island by combining an appeal to superstition with white man's cunning: "*His features are typically negroid, yet there is something decidedly distinctive about his face—an underlying strength of will. . . . His eyes are alive with a keen, cunning intelligence.*" He has cynically exploited the natives—"bush-niggers" he calls them—until they have rebelled, and he is forced to flee. Taking to the jungle to make his escape to a waiting warship, he loses his way, panics, and returns in a circle to the point of his entrance, where he is shot by the rebels. The factual story is simple, colorful, and relatively unimportant. It is told in three realistic scenes—the first two, and the eighth, or the last one of the play.

The central five scenes of the play all occur "*In the Forest. Night.*" They combine the reality of the actual jungle with the confused fantasy of Jones's mind. And all are illumined by the moon, which casts its doubtful light on scenes of re-enacted memory—partly from the actual past of Jones's life, and partly from the racial past of the Negro people. First, he meets a man he had once killed in a crap game, and kills him again; next, he meets the foreman of a chain gang whom he also had killed. Then "*a big dead stump worn by time into a curious resemblance to an auction block*" becomes the imagined scene of a Southern slave-auction; and then dead logs become the bodies of slaves in the hold of a ship. Finally, *"at the foot of a gigantic tree by the edge of a great river,"* he sees *"a rough structure of boulders like an altar."*——"Seems like I been heah befo'," he imagines. A witch doctor appears and dances, and a monstrous crocodile crawls from the river toward Jones. In final panic Jones shoots the monster, and the scene suddenly shifts to the daylight reality of the outside world. There the Negro rebels have, in fact, shot the emperor Jones.

The fascination of the play lies in its combination of daylight reality with moonlight illusion. Jones not only flees through the actual jungle to his death, but returns through the forest of the mind to his own past, and to the collective unconscious. And the crocodile which he kills becomes a symbol of the evil, both of his own nature and of all mankind. But this primitive monster is also a symbol of his own inner-most self; its death coincides with his own.

Obviously O'Neill constructed this drama of delusion and dream with conscious intent. The hero's regression through individual memory to the racial unconscious is too clearly patterned to be accidental. And there had been many prototypes of it in the literature of the day: Jack London's primitivistic heroes, particularly, had "been there before." The psychological theories of Carl Jung, with their quasi-religious interpretation of the psychology of the unconscious, also influenced O'Neill at this time. *The Emperor Jones* is both a drama of physical primitivism and one of the subconscious soul of man. But the greatness of the play lies in its very lack of explicitness, and in the dramatic unity and skill of its conception and realization.

Two dramatic devices succeed in unifying the separate scenes of the play, and in fusing the physical and the psychological elements of it. The steady background beating of the tom-tom has become famous. Beginning in the first scene, *"It starts at a rate exactly corresponding to normal pulse beat—72 to the minute —and continues at a gradually accelerating rate from this point uninterruptedly to the very end of the play."* Realizing artistically the union of physical and psychological, it produces a quasi-musical effect much like that of Ravel's *Bolero,* and ends suddenly with the shooting of the emperor at the end of the play. Synchronized with the tom-tom, the six shots from the emperor's revolver—ending with the shooting of the magic silver bullet at the end—punctuate the scenes of the play. Each shot is both physical and psychological, dramatizing some former act of violence, and some present discharge of hatred or of panic. Having told the "bush niggers" that only a silver bullet could ever kill him, the emperor himself uses a silver bullet to kill the symbolic crocodile of his primitive fears; and the rebels use an actual bullet made of "money" to kill the actual emperor. These dramatic and symbolic devices have made this "the most perfectly theatrical of all O'Neill's plays."

Yet *The Emperor Jones* is never merely theatrical. Its fundamental themes are those of human life itself—the eternal conflict of good and evil, of sunlight and moonlight, of civilization and savagery, of the clearing and "the Great Forest." *"In the rear the forest is a wall of darkness dividing the world."* The drama tells once again the archetypal myth of *The Heart of Darkness,* and may have been inspired partly by Conrad's novel of that name. Its hero is a perfect mixture of the dual opposites of man's nature. "The progress of Jones," Doris Falk has suggested, "is the progress in self-understanding, it is the striking off of the masks of the self, layer by layer, just as bit by bit his 'emperor's' uniform is ripped from his back, until in the end he must confront his destiny—himself—in nakedness." But Jones never does quite understand his true self, although his audience does. His tragic grandeur is rather that of the romantic absolutist who wears his emperor's mask to the bitter end. The concluding speech of Smithers explains his romantic heroism: "Silver bullets! Gawd blimey, but yer died in the 'eighth o' style, any'ow!"

Yet even this ending seems somewhat theatrical. The underlying characterization and structure of the play suggest a deeper significance and a greater dramatic art than are apparent. The play prefigures both the basic theme and the structure of O'Neill's final, great plays. Like Hickey of *The Iceman Cometh,* Jones attempts to live without illusions: his cynical intelligence has rejected all the romantic sentiments of life, and he has attempted to manipulate "nigger superstitions" to his own end. But his great illusion is the belief that he can live without illusions, and his denial of romantic idealism becomes a denial of life itself. Like the self-deluded Hickey, he dies in the tangled jungle of his own mind, destroyed by his imperial self-superiority.

The structure of the play, finally, prefigures that of *Long Day's Journey into Night*. The dramatic progression of the action in present time counterpoints the dramatic regression of the memory into time past, which in turn develops a progressive understanding of the psychological motivation within the mind. *The Emperor Jones*, on its primitive level, also dramatizes a "long day's journey into night," which advances in physical action, as it regresses in psychological action, until it ends symbolically in an illumination of the heart of darkness within the soul of man. The difference is that the primitive "emperor" never fully comprehends his own tragedy, and can never transcend it. He dies as he has lived, the confused victim of his own past, lost within "the Great Forest."

IV   Anna Christie

Anna Christie, produced exactly one year after *The Emperor Jones*, proved almost as popular. It was enthusiastically reviewed, and it ran for 117 performances, and it won for its author his second Pulitzer Prize. It was quickly made into a silent movie, and in 1929 was remade into a "talkie," with Greta Garbo in the title role. Thirty-three years later a large jury of film critics at the Seattle World's Fair voted this one of the fourteen best motion pictures ever produced in America. And this cinematic excellence suggests a reason for the play's popularity: it is one of the most perfectly romantic of O'Neill's early works. But the fact that both *Beyond the Horizon* and *Anna Christie* won Pulitzer Prizes, while two much better plays of the same period—*The Emperor Jones* and *Desire Under the Elms*—were passed by, suggests an ironic commentary on official taste.

In spite of its popularity *Anna Christie* suffers from obvious faults, which were emphasized by George Jean Nathan before the play was produced. Written by fits and starts, it lacked unity. Two years before final production an earlier version had been tried out in Atlantic City under the title of *Chris*. In this play the character of Anna's father had dominated, while both Anna and her lover remained minor. After several attempts at revision, O'Neill finally withdrew the early play, and later rewrote it with a newly conceived Anna in the title role. But in the process the center of action had shifted, the characters had changed, and the ending had become doubtful. Popular critics, of course, were delighted to find an O'Neill play that seemed to end happily. But many condemned its "sentimentalism," and O'Neill, after several attempts to defend it, finally decided against the play. In 1932 he stipulated that it must not be included in the selection of his best *Nine Plays*.

The main plot describes the conflict of Chris Christopherson, the captain of a small barge, and his daughter Anna. He has tried to protect her from "dat ole davil, sea," by having her brought up by cousins far inland in Minnesota. But, unknown to him, one of these cousins has seduced her, and she has drifted into prostitution. Now she visits him in New York for the first time, and he sees with dismay that she loves the sea. He tries bitterly to prevent this love and also her love for a young Irish sailor, Mat Burke. Finally she tells him the truth about her own past, and he reacts by getting drunk and signing on an ocean-going ship. Like his prototype, the "square-'ead" Olson of the *S. S. Glencairn*, he succumbs to his destiny as homeless child of the sea.

Meanwhile the sub-plot describes the love affair of Anna and Mat Burke, the sailor. Immediately attracted to him, she nevertheless realizes that he may cease to love her if he learns about her past. But she forces herself to tell him, as well as her father, declaring that she has never really loved anyone before him. He also reacts by getting drunk and signing (by chance) on the same ship as her father. But, when Mat finally returns to confront her again, he becomes convinced of her true love. At the conclusion they go off to marry, knowing that on the next day he must leave on "the long voyage" away from home. Love triumphs, but the future remains bleak.

The character of Chris, "childishly self-willed and weak, of an obstinate kindliness," is one of O'Neill's minor triumphs. Without any understanding of himself and without any realistic love or responsibility for this daughter whom he has never seen for fifteen years, he yet imagines that merely by shielding her from the sea he can protect her. In his "obstinate kindliness" he seems the perfect foil for the earlier "emperor" Jones, with his equally obstinate worldliness. But the character of Mat Burke, at the other extreme, is that of a romantic Irishman whose primitive innocence and blind love for Anna never seem quite credible. The romantic unreality of Mat weakens the play.

Between the realistic Chris and the unrealistic Mat stands Anna Christie. Unlike Chris, her character had developed very slowly in O'Neill's imagination; but, unlike that of Mat, it is now fully realized. Its complexity foreshadows the later characters of O'Neill's major plays, who seem both realistic and archetypal. Moreover, Anna is that typical figure of modern literature—the prostitute with a heart of gold. She possesses a clear intelligence which sees through the childish illusions of her father, and a perfect integrity which will not let her deceive her lover. Like Dostoevski's ideal prostitute in *Crime and Punishment*, Anna seems to stand above the sordid world and to become an instrument for its salvation. Also like Dostoevski's heroine, she has been called "sentimental." Why should a girl so pure in heart have taken to prostitution in the first place?

The character of Anna is crucial. She is drawn from life, but is larger than life. Like Dostoevski, O'Neill knew his prostitutes: her speech and her mannerisms are wholly convincing. And the actual details of her regeneration from the effects of her past are copied from letters of the former mistress of O'Neill's best friend, Terry Carlin. But beyond this, the deeper motivation of Anna's prostitution is derived from O'Neill's own psychological experience. Her childhood neglect by her father, her loneliness in alien surroundings, her seduction by a relative, and her drifting into prostitution—all reflect O'Neill's own feeling of desertion by his own parents, his loneliness at boarding school, the influence of his own brother, and the resulting profligacy of his own youth. The central theme of the play is the irresponsibility of Anna's father, which for a time drove the heroine into prostitution, but it did not destroy her.

Like the character of Anna, the ending of the play has been criticized for its mixed nature. It is not tragic, but it is true to life. Replying to criticism, O'Neill wrote: "It would have been so obvious and easy . . . to have made my last act a tragic one. It could have been done in ten different ways. . . . But looking deep into the hearts of my people, I saw that . . . they would act in just the silly, immature, compromising way that I have made them act."⁴ The play is not a tragedy, and should not be damned for its "failure" as one. Like the later *Strange Interlude,* it is a serious study of modern life, which dramatizes that mixture of comedy and tragedy most characteristic of life. Even for O'Neill, life was not always pure tragedy.

The apparent confusion and distiny of *Anna Christie* may be resolved by considering it as a serious romantic drama of character. The three central characters are all children of the sea, and each grows to understand and to accept his destiny. Anna has not only become regenerated by the sea, but has learned to accept her own past. Chris has stopped fighting the sea, and mutely accepts Anna's final assurance: "It's all right, Mat. That's where he belongs." And Mat agrees: "'Tis the will of God, anyway." At the end they all drink: "Here's to the sea, no matter what!" Obviously none of them is happy, and none expects happiness. Chris exclaims at the end: "Fog, fog, fog, all bloody time!" But they remain true to their inner natures, and they at last "belong."

V The Fountain

The Fountain was written immediately after *Anna Christie;* and, although it was not produced until 1925, its romantic theme and mood link it to the earlier plays. Although it failed on the stage, its poetic language gives clear expression to the romantic idealism of the early plays. It marks not only the end of a period in O'Neill's development but also the beginning of a new one. It was a poetic drama of a particular kind, intended for what O'Neill called, somewhat hopefully, "the theatre of to-morrow." Like *Marco Millions* and *Lazarus Laughed,* it attempted to fuse poetic myth with realistic action. If it failed dramatically, it still remains of considerable interest when considered as imaginative drama intended primarily for reading.

The Fountain attempted to dramatize romantic idealism in all its aspects. The plot follows the career of Juan Ponce de Leon, "soldier of iron——and dreamer," from youth, through age, to death. In the course of this career he successively embodies the different aspects of romantic idealism which the individual heroes of the earlier plays had embodied separately. In youth (like the Emperor Jones) Juan seeks power and wealth in order to build the empire of Spain. In "Scene Three: *Twenty years or so later,*" having become governor of Porto Rico, he finds life dull and aimless. Therefore (like Robert Mayo), he dreams of new adventure exploring the fabulous land: "Cathay, Cipango, who knows——." Moreover, the daughter of the woman he had once loved now arrives (like Anna Christie) to inspire new love, and he romantically seeks "the fountain of youth" which is fabled to flow in the new land. Finding this impossible fountain with the help of Indian guides, he is ambushed by them as he stoops to drink from it; and, pierced by arrows, he is left for dead. This much is romantic tragedy.

But mixed throughout this tragedy are passages of a romantic mysticism of a particularly naïve kind. The ideal heroine (first mother, and then daughter) named Beatriz (symbolizing the saving power of feminine beauty and love) repeatedly sings variations of a theme song:

> Life is a flower
> Forever blooming.
> Life is a fountain
> Forever leaping
> Upward to catch the golden sunlight,
> Striving to reach the azure heaven;
> Failing, falling,
> Ever returning
> To kiss the earth that the flower may live.

When Juan is ambushed beside the fountain, a voice seems to sing above him, and its inspiration calls him back to life. In the final scene, after he has returned to Porto Rico, he hears the song once again; it is sung this time by the young Beatriz to her young lover, his nephew. In final mystic ecstasy he realizes: "I am that song," and recognizes that the true "fountain of youth" is the eternal recurrence of youth, not in the individual, but in the race. "O Fountain of Eternity, take back this drop, my soul!" he exclaims, and dies.

Dramatically, the faults of the play are obvious. The characters seem mere symbols that lack the breath of life. O'Neill partly admitted this flaw when he noted in the program of the produced play: "Juan Ponce de Leon, in so far as I have been able to make him a human being, is wholly imaginary."[5] And the language which the characters speak is often stilted—not quite poetry, but too unrealistic to be prose. Partly, these faults resulted from attempting to naturalize myth and legend in the practical theater. But the later *Marco Millions* and *Lazarus Laughed* succeeded to a degree in overcoming these same faults.

The basic flaw in *The Fountain* lies deeper, in the confusion of its dramatic conception and of the mysticism which inspired it. Although the hero is both "soldier of iron and dreamer," the conflict of these opposites within his mind never becomes real. The vague inclusiveness of his nature blunts the conflict which had been sharp within Robert Mayo's nature, and which became sharp in the objective opposition of Marco Millions and the Great Kaan. Moreover, the romantic hero who experiences ecstasy beside the fountain of youth does not die. His mystic vision miraculously saves him and allows him a happy old age, freed from tragedy. Edwin Engel has remarked that "the romantic dream pays off," and he has compared this romantic mysticism to that of Emerson's "Brahma." But true mysticism never "pays off" physically: when it is dramatized realistically, "the slain" (if not "the slayer") suffers tragedy. The plot of *The Fountain* confuses the romantic dream with true mysticism. Later, *Lazarus Laughed* would avoid this basic confusion, and describe mysticism more realistically—and more eloquently.

CHAPTER 4

From *The Ape* to *Marco*: Reaction

I The Hairy Ape

WHEN *The Hairy Ape* first opened on Broadway on April 17, 1922, O'Neill broke two long-standing precedents: he attended the Broadway opening of one of his own plays, and he dressed for it in a formal dinner jacket. As the audience began assembling, the reason for this became apparent. A colorful group entered the theater, and "one man, who wore a loud check suit and a blazing red tie, said to O'Neill: 'Glad to see you, pal. You look great in fish and chips.' "[1] The author had invited his old friends from the waterfront to see this new play about stokers and sailors and to witness his triumph with it. To his old shipmates and drinking companions he dramatically demonstrated that he had arrived. And they appreciated this, and also the evidence of his continuing friendship.

But there is irony in O'Neill's choice of this particular play for this demonstration. *The Hairy Ape* tells how "Yank," a brutish but heroic stoker, leaves his place in the bowels of the ship, tries to crash society, but discovers that he can never "belong." The play marks the beginning of O'Neill's long war with the soul-destroying materialism of American society. Soon the great god Brown would symbolically destroy the creative Dion Anthony, and Marco Millions would disgust the great Kaan. Only at the very end of O'Neill's career would Mike and Josie Hogan take their revenge upon the materialistic T. Stedman Harder of Standard Oil. But now "Yank," the symbolic brain-child of an Irish immigrant's son who had in fact "arrived," began his long fictional struggle to "belong," while the character in the loud check suit and the red tie declaimed: "You look great in fish and chips."

The Hairy Ape describes the failure of the uneducated American to "belong" to civilized society. In this drama about an idea—both the hero and the heroine remain symbols—"Yank" both looks and acts like a "hairy ape," while the social Mildred is described as an *"incongruous artificial figure."* "Yank" is always smudged with symbolic *"black,"* while Mildred is *"dressed all in white."* Yank speaks a dialect so ungrammatical that it sometimes becomes grotesque, while Mildred and her friends speak with the exaggerated artificiality of a Sunday supplement. Almost by definition, the primitive hero can never "belong" to the super-civilized heroine: the title, the characterization, the dialogue, the scenery, and the stage directions all emphasize this. The remarkable fact is that so unrealistic a play should succeed as well as this one does.

The Hairy Ape marks the beginning of O'Neill's long period of experimentation with the techniques of anti-naturalism. Its first stage direction declares that: *"the treatment of this scene, or of any other scene in the play, should by no means be naturalistic."* And the play borrows many of the techniques of the German expressionistic drama of the time. Like Karel Capek's *R. U. R.* and Elmer Rice's *The Adding Machine,* the characters are not so much symbols as intentionally unrealistic mechanisms. The churchgoers are *"A procession of gaudy marionettes, yet with something of the relentless horror of Frankensteins in their detached mechanical unawareness."* And this anti-naturalism reaches its dramatic climax when Yank *"lets drive a terrific swing, his fist landing full on the fat gentleman's face. But the gentleman stands unmoved as if nothing had happened."* Although the published stage directions did not specify masks, these "marionettes" in the actual performance had, with the aid of gauze and collodion, mask-like faces. And, of course, the gorilla, who ends the play by clutching "the hairy Ape" in his lethal embrace, wore the most complete mask of all.

Obviously the play gains much of its power from its conscious use of new expressionistic techniques. Like *R. U. R.* it dramatizes the mechanization of the modern world. But O'Neill was never at his best in dealing with self-conscious ideas—he was rather a dramatist of the emotions. And his "Yank," although frequently directed to sit *"brooding, in as near to the attitude of Rodin's 'the thinker' as he can get*," simply cannot "t'ink." But he can feel. And his feelings sometimes seem to distort the neat patterns of the expressionistic drama.

The plot describes the progressive emotional involvement of the hero with the complex relationships of modern society. At the beginning in the stokehole, he proclaims his importance as part of the force that makes the engines go. And he emphasizes his superiority to Paddy, who dreams of the good old days of the sailing ships. But, when the white Mildred comes slumming and calls him a "filthy beast," he is so shocked that he determines to follow her into her own world. On "*a corner of Fifth Avenue in the Fifties on a fine Sunday morning*," he tries to talk with some churchgoers; but, finding that they ignore him, he furiously attacks them, and is sent to jail. There he hears that the revolutionary "I. W. W." is going to blow up society; but when he tries to join the I. W. W., his mindless violence is again rejected as completely as it had been by society itself. He progresses from shock to frustration to exasperation to despair; finally he can find comradeship only in the arms of the gorilla at the zoo. The action follows a steady progression, and the emotional violence of the hero is partially realized by means of the action and the dialogue.

The trouble is that the emotional violence of the hero and his sudden alienation from American life are not fully motivated nor explained. When audiences failed fully to appreciate the play, O'Neill complained: "Yank is really yourself, and myself. . . . But apparently very few people seem to get this." And to O'Neill, Yank was truly "myself"—he was the eternal outsider and alien. But to the average, native-born American, the violence of Yank's feeling of alienation seemed excessive. By definition, a character named "Yank" should have "belonged" partly to American life.

Originally, O'Neill had written *The Hairy Ape* as a short story, with the hero as an Irishman. But, when he rewrote it as a play, he converted his Irish hero into the symbolic "Yank," and thereby cut him off from his roots in actual experience. For the hairy ape, the eternal outsider, should have been named Driscoll, or Paddy, or Tyrone, or Hogan, rather than Yank. In his next play, O'Neill went to the opposite extreme, and made his hero Jim Harris, a Negro.

II All God's Chillun Got Wings

All God's Chillun Got Wings seems, on the surface, a drama of race relations. Because it dramatized the marriage of a Negro man and a white woman, its production caused a sensation, and New York censors persecuted it by denying licenses to some of its actors. This action only caused more people to flock to see it; and, in spite of poor reviews from most of the critics, it enjoyed a *succès de scandale*. Later, combined with *The Emperor Jones*, it ran for more than a hundred performances. O'Neill himself continued to value it highly. And, when European critics and producers praised it as a courageous study of American race relations, it achieved status. Yet the play is much more—and much less—than a sociological drama of race relations.

Superficially a tragedy of miscegenation, *All God's Chillun* is fundamentally another tragedy of alienation—like *The Hairy Ape* —and another symbolic study of the destructive effect of a materialistic society. It dramatizes the tragic failure of Jim "Crow" Harris to "belong"—either to his white wife, or to the white man's society. It emphasizes the devious ways in which this society prevents the true union of Negro and white. As a child Ella Downey had genuinely loved Jim Harris, but their friends of both races had ridiculed and opposed this love. "You aimin' to buy white?" a Negro taunts Jim. And later Ella is seduced by one of her white "friends" and, later still, turns to prostitution. But Jim doggedly hopes to marry her: "I don't ask you to love me—I don't dare to hope nothing like that." Finally and in desperation Ella accepts him. But now Jim's mother and sister oppose this marriage to a fallen woman, and Ella, torn between love and hate, finally goes insane. Her hatred of the black in him, in turn, causes him to fail his examinations for the law. At the end she regresses into a childlike dementia: "I'll be just your little girl, Jim—and you'll be my little boy—just as we used to be, remember, when we were beaux, and I'll put shoe blacking on my face, and pretend I'm black, and you can put chalk on your face and pretend you're white just as we used to do. . . ." And he finally finds a kind of salvation in caring for this child-like wife.

The hero and heroine of this play bear the familiar given names of Eugene O'Neill's mother and father, "Jim" and "Ella," and it has been pointed out that they act out some of the tragic conflicts later dramatized in *Long Day's Journey*.[2] Clearly there is some relationship between the psychological conflicts of this play and of O'Neill's own family life. Jim Harris, beyond his Negro race, is a symbolic embodiment of the "black" or dark side of man's nature, which conflicts with the "white" or socially acceptable side. This actual conflict continues not only the black and white symbolism of *The Hairy Ape*, but also its emphasis on alienation: "*In the street leading left the faces are all white; in the street leading right, all black.*" And Ella Downey's tragic regression into a childlike insanity also foreshadows Mary Tyrone's dope-dream of childhood innocence. The play is rich in symbol and psychological suggestion.

But *All God's Chillun* is so overlaid with a variety of symbol that it fails to focus clearly. Unlike "the hairy ape," Jim "Crow" Harris is not simply the black outcast, or the uneducated worker. And unlike "the emperor Jones," he is not simply the "black" materialist. It is Jim's father who suggests Brutus Jones: "*an elderly negro with an able, shrewd face but dressed in outlandish lodge regalia.*" The father has already made his fortune, and now Jim is striving, not for material success, but for acceptance and status. And he is hopelessly confused by his ambiguous position.

Paradoxically, the love of Jim Harris for Ella Downey is described as a kind of bloodless adoration, and their marriage becomes that of brother and sister—the exact opposite of the lurid "miscegenation" which the seekers of social sensation had anticipated. As it develops, the play becomes neither the simple study of race relations which it first seemed, nor even the symbolic study of the conflict of black and white which it is in part. Rather, it becomes a case history of abnormal psychology. By dramatizing the mental conflicts within the minds of Jim and Ella, the play points to the major psychological dramas to come. But its limited scope and its mixed techniques prevent its full realization.

The faults of the play are obvious. Although it is brief and consists of a quick succession of seven scenes (like *The Emperor Jones* and *The Hairy Ape*), it covers a period of seventeen years; and it follows the transformations of its characters from childhood through adolescence to middle age. Although its theme is complex, describing ambiguous emotions and subconscious thoughts (like those of *Strange Interlude*), it lacks both the scope and the skill necessary to realize these. It achieves neither unity, nor dramatic conviction.

Moreover, *All God's Chillun* fails to achieve tragic stature. Its hero lacks not only the courage to face his problems, and the heroism to fight against them, but also the self-knowledge to understand them. He is, instead, a disturbed personality, whose psychology is abnormal and whose failure is pathetic rather than tragic. And Ella Downey reflects both the frustrations and the confusions of her lover. Like the earlier Anna Christie, she is weak and embittered; but, unlike Anna, she can achieve neither true love nor self-understanding. Although she recognizes the goodness of Jim and calls him "the only white man in the world," she cannot love him; and she is driven to vent her own self-hatred upon him and his race. And, although her feeling of sub-conscious hatred for him is justified psychologically by his own masochistic self-abasement before her (he desires only "to become your slave! yes, be your slave—your black slave that adores you as sacred"), their joint confusion excludes the possi-bility either of true love or of heroism. The depth of genuine feeling, which distinguishes all of O'Neill's best plays, is absent in this one.

Worst of all, the ending of *All God's Chillun Got Wings*, with the spiritual meaning which its title implies, rings false. When Ella becomes insane and regresses into a childish dependence upon Jim, he becomes suddenly exalted. Although he has earlier blasphemed against God, he now realizes that Ella's insanity has freed her of hatred for him, and has given him the total responsibility of caring for her—as her "slave." Therefore he "*suddenly throws himself on his knees and raises his shining eyes, his transfigured face*: 'Forgive me God—and make me worthy . . .' *He begins to weep in an ecstasy of religious humility.*" And he ends: "(*still deeply exalted*) 'Honey, Honey, I'll play right up to the gates of Heaven with you!'" But the spiritual "wings" which "exalt" Jim Harris are not those of tragic understanding and self-transcendence; they are those of pathetic defeat and self-delusion.

The high point of the play—and its one genuinely tragic moment—is achieved by means of "*a primitive mask from the Congo—a grotesque face, inspiring obscure, dim, connotations in one's mind, but beautifully done, conceived in a true religious spirit."* Symbolizing the racial past of the Negro, this mask becomes for Ella Downey the embodiment of all the blackness which she hates; and, in the final scene, she *"grabs the mask from its place, sets it in the middle of the table and plunging the knife down through it pins it to the table."* Symbolically, she "strikes through the mask" to destroy the dark, inner self of her Negro husband, and thus precipitates the tragedy. The dramatic effect is brilliant, and the use of the mask to dramatize the psychological tragedy foreshadows *The Great God Brown.*

But this symbolic action seems also to have had an immediate effect on the mind of the author himself. "Strike through the mask!" Melville's Ahab had exhorted. And by making his white heroine strike through this Congo mask symbolizing the racial unconscious, O'Neill himself seems suddenly to have' gained access to his own unconscious. His next play, *Desire Under the Elms,* has been called "unconscious autobiography."[3] And quite suddenly and inexplicably, he achieved with it new success and power.

III   Desire Under the Elms

O'Neill once told Walter Huston that he had dreamed one night the whole of *Desire Under the Elms.* And the plot suggests many strange echoes of his own past familial experience. The father, Ephraim Cabot, wars constantly with his sons—as does the father of *Long Day's Journey*—and his "hardness" also suggests the parsimony of the autobiographical James Tyrone. In *Desire* the mother of Eben Cabot has recently died—as had the actual mother of Eugene O'Neill, and the son accuses the father of treating her badly—as does the son in *Long Day's Journey.* Finally, the dramatic conflict which precipitates the tragedy of *Desire* both reflects and distorts the one incident of O'Neill's early life which he omitted from *Long Day's Journey.* The young Eugene had divorced his first wife, and he had rejected the son born of the marriage. Now the love between the young heroine and the son is portrayed as unsanctioned, and she is made to kill her infant son in the deluded hope of proving her true love. O'Neill's early guilt and his fear of fatherhood perhaps found projection in this strange, elemental play, set on a New England farm of a century before.

The plot of *Desire* also re-enacts many of the tragic incidents of the old Greek myths. As in *Oedipus,* the son fights the father, and commits adultery (technically incest) with the mother (in this case, the step-mother). As in *Medea,* the wife kills her child in order (partly) to gain revenge on the husband. But the plot of *Desire* changes the pattern of the old Greek tragedies so radically that it creates an essentially new myth. Because the mother is now a third wife, and therefore a young step-mother to the mature son, the love of the two becomes wholly natural (though technically incestuous). And because the step-mother kills her infant because of a deluded (but genuine) love for the step-son, the cold violence of Medea's hatred is transformed into a warm love. A modern critic has complained that "if O'Neill's play has a kinship with *Oedipus,* it is with the complex rather than *Rex.*"[4] If this is partly true, the criticism implied is not. Because the plot of *Desire* creates a modern myth with new relationships, it suggests a new interpretation of the tragedy. Unlike *Mourning Becomes Electra, Desire* never pretended to domesticate classical myth in modern terms.

But the elemental violence of the plot of *Desire,* which recalled the violence of the old Greek myths but refused the sanctions of traditional Greek tragedy, disturbed many readers and critics when the play was first produced. In New York the censor demanded that a jury pass judgment on the morality of the play (it was duly acquitted). *Desire* was banned in Boston, of course, but it was also banned in Great Britain by the Lord Chamberlain. Later in Los Angeles the entire cast of the road company was arrested and tried on the charge of obscenity—and Hollywood was duly protected from sin. Even the first professional critics mostly failed to appreciate the play. But gradually, as thoughtful readers and critics increasingly admired it, its full stature became evident. Meanwhile, it enjoyed a long run (even if it attracted audiences for the wrong reasons); and it has often been revived, both on professional and amateur stages.

The plot of *Desire* may be described with equal accuracy from two points of view: that of the censor, and that of the modern critic. The play opens in 1850, on the farm of Ephraim Cabot—a hard-working, God-fearing patriarch. His first two wives have died, and in the first act he has just left to bring home a third wife. His three sons hate him and plot against him, and Eben (the only son of the second wife) steals the father's money to buy the inheritance of his older brothers, who then run away to join the California gold rush, just as Ephraim and his bride, Abbie, return. The second act describes the increasing hatred of Abbie for her old husband, and her gradual seduction of the young Eben (she has married only to get the security of the farm). The act ends with the "incest" of "mother" and son. The third act begins a year later with a raucous party celebrating the birth of a new son (all the guests know that it is actually not Ephraim's but Eben's). But young Eben learns that Abbie has seduced him to father a new heir who will insure her own inheritance of the farm. He denounces her, and she smothers their infant to prove that her love for Eben was not calculating but real. In his disbelief he informs the sheriff. But in the final scene he is convinced of her love, and he accepts his share of blame for the crime. The young lovers are led to their punishment, and old Ephraim is left alone on his farm.

The censor emphasized the hatred and vengeance of the sons, the theft of the father's money by the son, the incest of mother and son, and the infanticide. But the modern critic emphasizes rather the motives and the circumstances of these actions. The father was a tyrant, who had worked his wives to death; the money stolen by the son had rightfully belonged to his own mother; the incest was technical only, and at worst was adultery; and finally, the infanticide was the only true crime. Of their adultery, Abbie affirms: "I don't repent that sin!" And Eben agrees: "Nor me—but it led up t' the other——an' the murder ye did, ye did on account of me——an' it's my murder too." Therefore at the end the two lovers stand united—even exalted by the recognition of their true love: *"they both stand for a moment looking up raptly in attitudes strangely aloof and devout."* Is this sentimental immorality, or tragic exaltation?

The play refuses to judge—and therein lies much of its greatness. The alternatives are presented in terms of dramatic action and dialogue, not of the author's stage directions. Unlike its predecessors, *Desire* does not merely denounce materialism (embodied in Ephraim Cabot) and exalt the natural man (embodied in Eben Cabot). For once, the antagonists are evenly matched. The tragedy transcends the dramatic idea which it seems to illustrate.

The hero of *Desire*, and the apparent spokesman of its author, has often seemed to be the sensitive son, Eben Cabot. Like his dead mother, he has been mistreated and misunderstood by his tyrannical father. His older brothers like him, his stepmother loves him, all the neighbors sympathize with him, and everyone agrees in fearing and hating the old man. This violent and explicit hatred of Ephraim Cabot, indeed, seems to have shocked the censor as much as anything. At the climax of the first act the oldest son imitates *"his father's voice*: 'I'm ridin' out t' learn God's message t' me in the spring like the prophets done,' he says. I'll bet right then and thar he knew plumb well he was goin' whorin', the stinkin' old hypocrite!" By contrast, the tragic exaltation of the young lovers which concludes the play is described as "raptly devout."

But over the years it has gradually become apparent that the true "hero" of *Desire* is not young Eben, but old Ephraim Cabot. The old man not only dominates the action of the play, but also emerges as its most memorable character—and one of the greatest of its author's dramatic creations. Ephraim may seem a tyrant and a hypocrite to others, but to himself he is the chosen instrument of an Old Testament God. " 'God's hard, not easy! God's in the stones! Build my church on a rock——out o' stones an' I'll be in them! . . . I'd made thin's grow out o' nothin'——like the will o' God, like the servant of His hand. It wa'n't easy.' " His New England theodicy—both historically and psychologically true—gives Ephraim a towering stature, and an inward reality far greater than that of his sons or relations. It is an embodiment of the *hubris* of Greek tragedy, but it is also an embodiment of the highest heroism of modern man: Milton's "courage never to submit or yield,/And what is else not to be overcome."[5]

Like Milton's Samson and Satan, Ephraim Cabot is heroic; like them also, he is an instrument of evil, and of the destruction of others. He remains a tyrant, utterly self-righteous, who seeks to possess both the farm and the youth of others wholly for himself. He is the incarnation of ownership—the spokesman of a materialistic society which destroys the souls of other men. Therefore he is hated. But—and this is the important point—he is also respected. He is recognized as the embodiment of the human will to power, which creates the values of the material world. The play ends, not with the tragic exaltation of Eben and Abbie, nor even with the grim heroism of Ephraim, but with the casual and impersonal comment of the Sheriff: "(*looking around at the farm enviously—to his companion*) 'It's a jim-dandy farm, no denyin'. Wished I owned it!'"

In the deepest sense, neither Eben nor Ephraim Cabot is the hero of *Desire*. The final hero is the spirit of Nature. The play finally becomes a kind of dramatic fable which realizes the abstract truth of Emerson's poem, "Hamatreya." Throughout, the Earth-Spirit seems to sing: "Mine—not yours./Earth endures." The older brothers: *"shoulder each other . . . like two friendly oxen toward their evening meal."* And Ephraim Cabot escapes from the house to sleep with the animals in the barn (O'Neill himself sometimes escaped from the company which his wife invited by sleeping in the barn). Abbie warns her lover: "Nature'll beat ye, Eben." And the title of the play emphasizes this fact. In different vein, Abbie warns Ephraim about the farm: "Ye can't take it with ye!" And O'Neill seems instinctively to have returned to the simple, naturalistic style of his early plays to give simple, direct expression to this elemental tragedy.

Almost unconsciously, and with little critical fanfare, *Desire Under the Elms* seems to have impressed itself on the modern mind. And on January 11, 1963, as this chapter was being written, a new revival by Jose Quintero was reviewed in the New York *Times*: "If you think that Eugene O'Neill's *Desire Under the Elms* is old-fashioned and creaky, go down to Bleecker Street, in Greenwich Village."

IV The Great God Brown

After completing *Desire Under the Elms,* O'Neill worked simultaneously on two plays; but he completed *The Great God Brown* before *Marco Millions,* and the play was both published and produced first. Both plays carried forward his attack on the materialism of modern society. Brown (as O'Neill specifically explained) "is the visionless demi-god of our new materialistic myth——a Success——building his life on exterior things, inwardly empty. . . ." *Marco Millions* would translate this "new materialistic myth" to the ancient Orient. But "Billy Brown" was one hundred percent American.

The Great God Brown is one of the most interesting but also one of the most confusing of O'Neill's plays. It contains some of his most challenging dramatic ideas and some of his most original characters. Moreover, it achieved success at the time of production, and it was both praised and reproduced throughout the civilized world. It marks a milestone in O'Neill's career, and it also prepared the way for his later triumphs. But it remains a strangely artificial play. Mixing dramatic experimentation with self-conscious poetry, genuine insight with bookish theory, this play attempted everything, but achieved final success with nothing. At the time it seemed greater than *Desire Under the Elms*, but now its fireworks seem contrived.

The element of artificiality in *The Great God Brown* is illustrated by the simple summary of its plot. The first two acts describe the tragedy of Dion Anthony—the sensitive artist who finds himself in conflict with a materialistic society. He has married, and the need of supporting a wife and three sons has forced him to give up his painting and he takes to drink. His wife gets him a job as a draftsman in the architectural office of his old classmate, William A. Brown. But he feels humiliated, and seeks solace and understanding in the arms of Cybel, the eternal prostitute. Lacking the true love of his wife and the true appreciation of his old friend and employer, he finally drinks himself to death.

The second two acts then describe the second tragedy—that of William A. Brown. After Dion's death, Brown assumes the "mask" of his former friend and employee, Dion Anthony. And with this mask he inherits Dion's ability to create, so that his architectural designs win him even greater success than before. With the mask he also wins the love of Dion's wife, who identifies him with her husband. But with the mask he tragically inherits Dion's bitter honesty and insight into the truth. And this honesty compels him to denounce the artistic falsity of his own architectural designs and to recognize the inner duplicity of his own divided personality. Finally, abandoning the "mask" of the insensitive William A. Brown, he also flees to the arms of Cybel, where the police find only the "mask" of Dion Anthony, whom they now accuse of "murdering" Billy Brown. The eternal artist and the eternal materialist have destroyed each other. At the end the police captain asks: "Well, what's his name?" And Cybel, the Earth Mother, replies: "Man!"

Taken together, Dion Anthony and Billy Brown represent the divided personality of modern man. They are, in one sense, two separate and opposing characters; in another, they are the conflicting aspects of the single character, "Man." Both the complexity and the confusion of the play lie in its uncertainty concerning these two alternatives. Dion Anthony and Billy Brown are brothers under the skin. But do they have two skins, or one? Are they really two people, or are they the conflicting halves of one person? And does *The Great God Brown* really consist of two plays, of two acts each? Or is it one play of four acts?

The Great God Brown became famous for its daring use of masks to suggest the conflicting personalities of each of its characters. Earlier, *The Hairy Ape* had painted on masks to emphasize the artificial "faces" of people in "Society." And later *Lazarus Laughed* used formal masks to define type characters. But in *The Great God Brown* all the characters used masks to dramatize the contrast between their external, or public selves, and their inner, or private selves. And this new use of masks suggested psychological complexities beyond the scope of the old, realistic drama.

But the trouble with *The Great God Brown* lies in the confusing ambiguity of its use of masks. At the beginning Dion's *"mask is a fixed forcing of his own face."* But as his tragedy develops, this mask becomes (first) the mask of "Pan," and (finally) the mask of "Mephistopheles." And after his death, Brown is able to assume at will Dion's "mask" (which one?). Meanwhile Brown wears no mask at first, but (at the end of the second act) he assumes Dion's; and (at the end of the fourth act) he discards his own *"mask of William Brown,"* and permanently assumes Dion's. Thereupon his associates proclaim that "Mr. Brown is dead!" And they *"return, carrying the mask of William Brown, two on each side, as if they were carrying a body by the legs and shoulders."* If this seems brilliantly imaginative, it is also dramatically confusing. The manipulation of a variety of masks tends to become mere hocus-pocus.

The Great God Brown succeeded on the stage in spite of its strange plot, and it continues to fascinate the reader despite its confusing use of masks. Its occasional excellence derives partly from its author's autobiographical insight, reflected in the action, and partly from his creative use of his wide reading. Dion's tragedy is clearly an allegory of O'Neill's own. Cybel tells him: "You're not weak. You were born with ghosts in your eyes and you were brave enough to go looking into your own dark." And at the other extreme, this "Dion Anthony" is clearly a mixture of Nietzsche's Dionysus and of Saint Anthony; "Cybel" is a mixture of the goddess Cybele, the earth mother, and the eternal prostitute; and Dion's wife Margaret is a modern embodiment of Faust's Margaret. At its best, the play partly realizes a modern myth; at its worst, it becomes a self-conscious allegory.

But if *The Great God Brown* suffers from artificiality of plot, from confusing use of masks, and from self-consciousness of allegory, it manages finally to make a virtue of these very faults. In the last analysis, the play achieves its moments of tragic greatness by means of its very incongruities and confusions. Cybel, for instance, *"chews gum like a sacred cow forgetting time with an eternal end."* And this grotesque mixture of incongruous metaphors suggests the confusion of the modern world—which, of course, the title of the play also suggests. Finally, a speech by Billy Brown, after he has "murdered" his former self, also suggests the final insight of the play into the confusion of the modern world: "Sssh! This is Daddy's bedtime secret for today: Man is born broken. He lives by mending. The grace of God is glue." The final "grace" of *The Great God Brown*, perhaps, lies in its symbolic joining of dissociated fragments of experience by the glue of the creative imagination.

V Marco Millions

Marco Millions is the twin of *The Great God Brown* in many ways. The play, completed in its first draft before *Brown*, was then actually two plays. But the producers procrastinated until O'Neill cut and combined the two parts into one. In character, Marco re-embodies in a different setting the "materialistic myth" of Brown, and the play continues O'Neill's attack on American materialism. (In the Epilogue Marco, *"dressed as a Venetian merchant of the later thirteenth century,"* is discovered sitting among the American audience, *"much as one of them."*) The chief difference between the two plays is that Marco's materialism contrasts with the spirituality of the Orient, while Brown's contrasts with the spirituality of the artist. Therefore, where *The Great God Brown* is a psychological drama of opposing character types, *Marco Millions* is a historical pageant of opposing civilizations.

Like *The Great God Brown, Marco* is a play in two parts. The first act describes the material growth of young Marco Polo, and tells of his travels to the Orient. The third act, which describes the spiritual growth of old Kublai Kaan, tells of his progressive disillusion and tragedy. Only in the second act do the two central characters confront each other, and even then the twain do not meet; rather, they define their differences. The first half of the play belongs to Marco; the second half, to the Great Kaan.

But unlike *The Great God Brown,* which develops the successive tragedies of Dion Anthony and William Brown in terms of continuous psychological drama, *Marco Millions* first develops the comedy of Marco Polo in terms of broad satire, and then the tragedy of Kublai Kaan in terms of poetic mysticism. The two halves of this play not only dramatize different characters, but use different techniques. Sometimes *Marco* uses pure social satire, comparable to Sinclair Lewis' *Babbitt*. But at other times the play becomes poetic and mystical in the manner of *The Fountain* and *Lazarus Laughed*. Although O'Neill employed effective theatrical devices (such as parallel actions and a divided stage) to dramatize this dualism, the emotional effect is often confusing. Did the author intend realistic satire? Or did he wish to create romantic myth?

The early scenes of *Marco* skip from Venice, where the young Marco is ridiculed for writing a love poem to Donata, to the countries of the East—Persia, India and China—where he progressively learns the ways of the world and to suppress his romantic idealism. A Tartar prostitute tells him: "Don't sell your soul for nothing. That's bad business." In a climactic scene, he, with brash self-assurance, confronts Kublai Kaan and drives a good bargain for the privileges of trading in his realm.

In the second act Marco progressively instructs the Kaan in the ways of Western materialism, while the Kaan's beautiful granddaughter, Kukachin, tragically falls in love with this "strange, mysterious dream-knight from the exotic West." And ironically, the roles of East and West seem now reversed. Marco expounds his "democratic" scheme that "taxes every necessity of life, a law that hits every man's pocket equally," and he repeals the "tax on excess profits. Imagine a profit being excess!" (But, considered realistically, this "democratic" scheme seems more Oriental than Western.) Meanwhile Kukachin romantically intercedes for her Western dream-knight; and, at her request, the Kaan allows Marco to return with his wealth to Venice, on the condition that on the way he deliver Kukachin to the Shah of Persia to be married. But Marco is instructed that every morning he must gaze deeply into her eyes. In a climactic scene of pure burlesque, Marco gazes into her love-lorn eyes, but can detect only the symptoms of bilious fever. Impervious to love and beauty, he returns to Venice with his millions.

In the final act the Great Kaan hears from Persia that Kukachin is dying of a broken heart. Meanwhile Marco, who has returned to Venice, is about to wed his fat Donata. His wedding guests exclaim at his magnificence, and Marco makes a burlesque speech in Chamber-of-Commerce style describing the wealth of the East. As the theater lights dim on the wedding feast, the figure of the Great Kaan is spotlighted on an upper level, as he sits viewing Marco's wedding through his crystal ball. He dashes the crystal to the floor, and *Instantly there is darkness and from high up in the darkness Kublai's voice speaking with a pitying scorn*: 'The Word became their flesh, they say. Now all is flesh! And can their flesh become the Word again?' " Although this scene may seem artificial in reading, its theatrical contrast is dramatically effective.

In the final scene Kukachin's death is reported to the Kaan, and he seeks religious solace from the priests of Tao, Confucius, Buddha, and Islam. The religions of the East attempt to offer consolation for the tragedy produced by the blind materialism of the West. But the Kaan, unmoved, exclaims: "Do not wound me with wisdom. Speak to my heart!" And his wise counselor answers: "Then weep, old man!" At the end the play achieves genuine tragic effect as the Great Kaan finds final comfort, which he had been unable to find in the "wisdom" of intellectual disillusion and knowledge, in deeply felt grief.

Thus *Marco Millions* alternates between scenes of comic satire and exaggeration, and contrasting scenes of poetic romance and tragedy. All these are played against an opulent background of Oriental pageantry. The early scenes set in the West seem dull, and Marco's character does not become interesting until contrasted with the romance of the East. The central scenes, in which he confronts the Kaan, often develop effective satire. But only at the end, when the wise Kaan accepts tragic defeat, does the play seem wholly real—and then the earlier exaggerations of satire and romance are only half forgotten. The character of Marco seems too gross; that of the Kaan too pure. The play remains a historical pageant rather than a true drama.

Marco Millions marks the last of a series of plays in which O'Neill contrasted either the simplicity or the beauty of man's natural instincts with the artificiality or the materialism of his society. "The Hairy Ape," Jim "Crow" Harris, Eben Cabot, Dion Anthony and Kublai Kaan, all heroically struggled against the materialistic ways of the world, and all suffered defeat. But each progressively learned to understand and, finally, to accept his own tragedy. By means of this final realization, each play achieved a measure of greatness, in spite of its dualism.

But the three major plays following these achieved a greater unity. In the "Prologue" of *Marco Millions,* the coffin of Kukachin is being carried from Persia to China for burial. And, as her caravan halts in the desert heat, a mysterious light seems to shine from her face: *"Her lips are seen to move*: 'Say this, I loved and died. Now I am love, and live. And living, have forgotten. And loving, can forgive.'"* Meanwhile: *"A sound of tender laughter, of an intoxicating, supernatural gaiety, comes from her lips and is taken up in chorus in the branches of the tree as if every harp-leaf were laughing in music with her. The laughter recedes heavenward and dies. . . ."* Mixed with the burlesque satire of Marco and the bookish philosophy of the Great Kaan, this supernatural laughter sounds somewhat incongruous. But from the lips of the mythical Lazarus, it will ring true.

CHAPTER 5

From *Lazarus* to *Electra*: Descent

I Lazarus Laughed

UNIQUE among O'Neill's dramas—and indeed, in all dramatic literature—is *Lazarus Laughed*. It marks a turning point in his career. In it he attempted what few authors—and fewer playwrights—have ever done: to create a *Paradiso*, or ideal image of man; and, what is more difficult, to dramatize this ideal in terms of human action. Although he did not fully succeed, he did create a memorable work of the dramatic imagination.

In all the earlier plays he had described heroes torn between two opposing forces, and he had designed dramas whose structure emphasized this inner dualism. A farmer dreamed of lands beyond the horizon, and sailors dreamed of home; Billy Brown tried to steal the ideal "mask" of Dion Anthony; and Marco Polo repressed his youthful dream in order to amass millions: all had been haunted by some inner division of their natures. Now *Lazarus Laughed* dramatized only the ideal. And O'Neill's next two major plays, although they did not dramatize any ideal, continued to realize a new unity of conception. *Strange Interlude* described a purgatory of human compromise; *Electra*, inferno of human depravity.

Not only did *Lazarus Laughed* imagine an ideal hero, and dramatize his ideal in action, but it employed all the experimental techniques which O'Neill had earlier developed to implement his "theatre of tomorrow." In *The Great God Brown* masks had defined the separate personalities of his central characters; now a multiplicity of masks defined a variety of national and psychological character types. *Marco Millions* had used theatrical groupings and a divided stage to suggest the conflicts of East and West; now *Lazarus Laughed* used hundreds of actors grouped in costumes and masks to suggest on the stage the conflict of civilizations and religions. *Brown* had been a morality play; *Marco* a kind of historical pageant; now *Lazarus* dramatized a new religious myth.

Lazarus Laughed, therefore, attempted a new kind of drama. It was not tragedy, although its story is tragic. It was not realistic, and certainly not naturalistic. When it was successfully produced on an amateur stage, it became a pageant of the imagination, enriched by an opulence of costumes, masks, and choral effects. And many of its speeches were stylized. The drama was designed to appeal to the imagination rather than to common sense. But, for this reason it has always seemed impracticable to the commercial theater. It remains essentially a "closet drama" whose most effective theater is that of the reader's mind. It asks comparison with Hardy's *The Dynasts* or with Goethe's *Faust,* Part II, rather than with realistic or conventional plays.

The plot of *Lazarus Laughed* recalls the imaginative sweep of *The Dynasts.* It dramatizes the "life" of Lazarus after he has been raised from the dead and after Jesus has been crucified. It moves from Judea to ancient Greece, and finally to Rome. Act One describes the reappearance of Lazarus among his family and neighbors, to whom he preaches the new gospel that "there is no death!" The second scene develops the conflict between his Christian followers and the Orthodox. Act Two moves to Athens, where Lazarus is hailed as the new incarnation of the God Dionysus. Then the second scene moves to Rome, where he proclaims his new gospel to the senators and legionnaires. Acts Three and Four finally focus on the personal struggle between the faith of Lazarus and the cynical disbelief of Tiberius and Caligula, by whom he is finally burned at the stake at "Dawn."

The development of the action is primarily psychological and ideal. Lazarus himself grows younger as the play advances. He progressively frees himself from the sorrows and illusions of his past life and advances in the assurance of his new faith. Meanwhile, his gospel develops also: in Judea he is identified with the "Nazarenes," but in Greece his gospel is merged with the worship of Dionysus, and in Rome it develops to suggest the other-worldly religions of the East.

Criticism of *Lazarus Laughed* takes two forms. The first condemns the religious conception, and the gospel, or ideas, which the hero proclaims. The second condemns the abstraction of the play, and the imperfect dramatization of its ideal myth. The criticism of O'Neill's religious conception has often been narrow and doctrinaire, but the criticism of his imperfect realization of his myth in dramatic terms is more valid. One can only answer that O'Neill attempted the impossible, and partially succeeded.

The character of Lazarus, as well as the mythical life which he lives, is wholly the conception of the playwright. The actual story of the raising of Lazarus is told very briefly in the Bible, and many authors have felt free to interpret it in many different ways.[1] Thus William Butler Yeats, in *Calvary*, conceived Lazarus as indignant that Christ had called him back from the peace of the dead; and Robinson Jeffers, in *Dear Judas*, conceived Lazarus as unaffected by emotion because he had been freed from the illusions of life. But O'Neill's Lazarus is wholly positive; he welcomes all life with joy, now that he has passed beyond the fear of death. That O'Neill should preach the wholesale affirmation of life, in contrast to his fellow-tragedians, and in contrast to his own "pessimistic" plays, seems paradoxical. The paradox is explained by the complexity of his conception.

The title *Lazarus Laughed* was chosen to contrast with the shortest verse in the Bible, "Jesus wept;" and these are the first two words spoken in O'Neill's play. Lazarus is intended as the counterpart of Jesus, and he now acts and preaches the joyous gospel of the resurrected Christ, in contrast to the tragic story of the crucified Christ. In origin and intention, Lazarus is Christian.

But *Lazarus* is also Greek and pagan, partly in origin and wholly in the dramatic second phase of his character. In the first act he seems partly Greek: *"His face recalls that of a statue of a divinity of Ancient Greece . . . in its detached serenity."* But in the second act he is wholly Greek: *"His countenance now might well be that of the positive masculine Dionysus, closest to the soil of the Grecian Gods, a Son of Man, born of a mortal."* Because O'Neill overlaid his fundamentally Christian idealism with the Grecian, his *Lazarus* has sometimes been called "pagan." And because he derived his conception of the Greek Dionysus from Nietzsche, his play has been said to preach the Nietzschean "superman."[2] But this Greek "paganism" is only one of the elements of the dramatic conception.

Throughout his life O'Neill had read widely in the literature of all religions. In *Marco Millions* he had quoted from the teachings of Buddhism and Taoism. Now he used elements of these Oriental religions in his conception of Lazarus, as Doris Alexander has pointed out.[3] His hero proclaims a religion of selflessness reminiscent of the Hindu scriptures: "Let a laughing away of self be your new right to live forever." His face is described as shining with an inner light, as in myths and paintings of the Buddha. His ideal of the passive acceptance of life, as illustrated by his refusal to prevent Miriam from eating the poisoned peach, recalls both Buddhism and the Oriental aspect of Christianity which preaches turning the other cheek. And the incident in which the dying lion licks Lazarus' hand is reminiscent of Buddhist mythology. These self-effacing, passive qualities of Lazarus certainly do not suggest a Nietzschean superman. O'Neill's hero embodies instead a religious ideal which includes elements of all the great religions of the world.

Lazarus dramatizes a modern religious idealism that is Christian in origin, Nietzschean in tragic conception, Oriental in mythology, but, perhaps, closest to the spirit of American Transcendentalism. In the first act Lazarus answers the question: "What did you find beyond there, Lazarus?" with Thoreau's words: "Is not one world in which you know not how to live enough for you?" Like the Transcendentalists, he also speculates: "What if there is no evil? What if there is only health and sickness?" And in modern terms his gospel develops the mysticism of Emerson's "Brahma": "Dying we laugh with the Infinite. We are the giver and the gift."

But Transcendental mysticism hardly seems likely material for modern tragedy. The astonishing fact is that *Lazarus Laughed* should succeed as well as it does in translating this idealistic material into dramatic terms. Its success is achieved partly by means of psychology, partly by dramatic incident and symbol, and partly by occasional passages of poetic eloquence.

The chief characters who oppose Lazarus are original in conception and well realized in action. His wife, Miriam, who loves him but cannot understand his new mystical faith, supplies the tragic foil for his optimistic exaltation: as he grows younger in his faith, she grows older in her earth-bound realism; finally she dies in his arms at the hands of the Romans. Tiberius Caesar, who puts Lazarus to death, is described as the cynical realist who knows the evil in men's hearts too well to see beyond it. But most interesting is Caligula; he dramatizes the pure evil which opposes the pure goodness of Lazarus: his is the sick soul of a spoiled child, who vacillates between a grudging admiration of Lazarus and a fear of the goodness which he can never understand.

To dramatize this conflict of ideal opposites, O'Neill has used a background of historical pageantry more sweeping than that of *Marco Millions*. And a series of vivid symbolic incidents serve to illustrate the larger themes. The most striking of these introduces Act Three: *"In the exact centre of the arch a cross is set up on which a full grown male lion has been crucified."* Above appears the inscription: *"From the East, land of false gods and superstition, this lion was brought to Rome to amuse Caesar."* When the dying lion licks Lazarus' hand, the double identity of the laughter of Lazarus with the religious mysticism of the East and with the tragic religion of Christ crucified is realized in the single, unforgettable image.

Interspersed with historical pageantry and with vivid incidents are passages in which Lazarus describes his own motivation and proclaims his gospel:

> In the dark peace of the grave the man called Lazarus rested. He was still weak, as one who recovers from a long illness—for, living, he believed his life a sad one! . . . He lay dreaming to the croon of silence, feeling as the flow of blood in his own veins the past re-enter the heart of God to be renewed by faith in the future. . . . Then, of a sudden, a strange gay laughter trembled from his heart as though his life, so long repressed in him by fear, had found at last its voice and a song for singing.

At its best the eloquence achieves the effect of poetry, and it translates the laughter into words. But O'Neill was too little the poet to succeed by means of eloquence alone.

When the Theatre Guild had finally decided against producing *Lazarus Laughed* because of the expense and the technical difficulties involved, O'Neill speculated on its future. If only

Chaliapin could be persuaded to play the part of Lazarus, singing the laughter in his magnificent operatic voice! In later years amateur groups have experimented in recording the laughter in musical cadences, and replaying it on the stage; but the result has seemed artificial. O'Neill subtitled *Lazarus Laughed, A Play for the Imaginative Theatre.* Perhaps in some theater of tomorrow, a combination of drama, opera, and pageantry may realize its potentialities. Who knows?

II   Strange Interlude

Strange Interlude proved as successful in the commercial theater as *Lazarus Laughed* was unsuccessful. It enjoyed the longest first run of any of O'Neill's plays in spite of excessive length and technical difficulties. The original Theatre Guild production ran for a year and a half on Broadway; a second cast, starring Judith Anderson, played "the provinces" with equal success. (As this chapter is being written, a Broadway revival by Jose Quintero is enjoying new success.) And, when the play was first published, it was read as if it were a novel by a vast audience (indeed, O'Neill had consciously designed and written the play on the analogy of the novel). Few works of similar scope have proved so popular.

But the very popularity of the play has caused many to distrust it: one critic even dubbed it "O'Neill's *Abie's Irish Rose.*" At the time of its first production, many condemned its "melodrama," and in modern times its explicit psychology has seemed to "date" it. But in 1928 both Nathan and Krutch hailed it as O'Neill's best, and the playwright himself never lost faith in it (as he did in other popular successes such as *Anna Christie*). It remains one of the most interesting and controversial of his productions. Is it a major drama, or a museum piece?

Like *Lazarus Laughed, Strange Interlude* has been condemned for not being what it did not intend to be—a conventional tragedy. But *Lazarus* had been ideal in conception and literary in execution. Now *Interlude* seemed merely a popular play. Neither its matter nor its manner was tragic: no character was killed, or even suffered very greatly. Admirers of O'Neill who expected high tragedy were disappointed, and detractors who had detected melodrama in all his plays found even more of it here. A recent review of its latest revival exclaims: "O'Neill's *Strange Interlude*: It's All of That!"

The play is best described, not as tragedy, nor even as realistic drama, but rather as a modern myth or morality play. Edwin Engel has suggested the title: "Everywoman." Its curious combination of symbolic melodrama with psychological realism constantly suggests overtones of myth. And its dramatic conception continues the logic of *Lazarus*: where the earlier play had been written from the point of view of the divine ideal, this one is written from the point of view of the all-too-human actual. The title itself emphasizes this middle ground: "our lives are merely strange dark interludes in the electrical display of God the Father."

The author's intention to describe a modern *Purgatorio* is emphasized further by the final words of Charlie Marsden to the heroine: "Let's you and me forget the whole distressing episode, regard it as an interlude, of trial and preparation, say, in which our souls have been scraped clean of impure flesh, and made worthy to bleach in peace." Although the language is that of scientific materialism, the conception is that of religious idealism. In this play O'Neill consciously described his vision of the mid-world of human life (much as Emerson did in his essay on "Experience"). He abandoned the ideal world of religious transcendence (recently imagined in *Lazarus*), and he abandoned the exalted tone of high tragedy (to which his readers had become accustomed). Neither heaven nor hell, neither tragedy nor comedy is dramatized here, but the dead average of human experience.

But, if *Strange Interlude* describes a kind of living purgatory (as its title implies, and as its position between *Lazaraus* and *Electra* suggests), it is not in the usual sense a religious play. Its movement of thought and of feeling is downwards—away from all hope, and into disillusion. Unlike the traditional *Purgatorio* which described the road up from Hell to Paradise, this play describes O'Neill's descent toward the depths. *Lazarus* had proclaimed man's possible transcendence of death and despair; *Interlude* denounced all romantic dreams of earthly bliss. And the negativism of the play disturbed, most of all, O'Neill's admirers (who had recognized the exaltation of his earlier dramas). Here is "death without transfiguration," they said; "there is nothing to worship."

But through the years audiences and readers have continued to be fascinated by *Strange Interlude*. In 1928 when the play was first produced in New York—it was banned in Boston, but was staged in a barn-like movie theater in suburban Quincy—curious audiences filled the place to capacity, and listened in fascinated attention throughout the long performances. The utter sincerity of the play carried conviction. A generation later, more sophisticated audiences at the New York revival of the play sometimes laughed at its melodramatic machinery and its clichés; but they continued to be fascinated. As Walter Kerr expressed it, these modern audiences seemed to "share the experience of helping a century to revisit its youth."[4] In spite of obvious flaws, the play continues to carry the conviction of reality—"this is the way it was."

Perhaps the play's very averageness and its lack of tragic exaltation constitute its greatest virtue. All the characters are middle-class Americans who consciously try to lead normal lives. Except for the heroine in the beginning, they are not "haunted heroes" who seek martyrdom (like Lazarus), or who commit murder (like the Mannons). They are men of good will who try to do what is right, but who find that the world of experience does not correspond to the moral idealism in which they have been educated. They compromise, they commit venial sins, but they all feel (in the words of Nina to Marsden) that "I haven't been such an awfully wicked girl, have I, Father?" Exactly because they are so average and so naïve, they seem the more real—most people are like that. A modern morality play of "Everywoman" may become as moving as a tragedy of an *Emperor Jones* or an *Electra*.

But to raise these ordinary characters to the level of literary significance requires some quality of insight or some development of technique beyond that of realistic drama. The new technical innovation of *Strange Interlude* allows the characters to speak their normally unspoken thoughts on the stage, so that the conflict of their hidden human motives with their conventional middle-class morality becomes dramatically clear. And these hidden motives, at first analyzed in the explicit language of clinical psychology, then become generalized by the heroine's imagination into a kind of myth. By means of a leisurely analysis resembling that of the psychological novel, the characters are realized in dramatic depth. And then this realism is converted into myth by the "strange, devious intuitions" of the heroine and her creator.

The first act of this nine-act play may illustrate both its virtues and its defects. Like all first acts, it introduces the characters and their problems, but its exposition is both more leisurely and more explicit than usual. The motivation is made clear by the spoken thoughts with which the characters supplement their conventional speeches. But, although the speaking of these thoughts becomes an easily acceptable dramatic innovation, the author uses psychological terms and makes too explicit a motivation that (in normal life) would not become clear until much later. Therefore both the language and the motivation often seem artificial. But these spoken thoughts often develop surprisingly dramatic conflicts between inner feelings and outer conventions, which give rise both to new insight and to rich dramatic irony. And, finally this inner conflict develops a myth true both of character and to religious psychology.

The play begins soon after World War I. The heroine has been prevented by a possessive and moralistic father from consummating her love for her fiancé, who was then killed in the war. Guilty and resentful, she accuses her father and proclaims her intention of nursing soldiers who have been crippled by the war—and of giving herself to them. Shocked, her father exclaims: "You're not yourself!" But Nina replies: "(*Her voice becoming a bit uncanny, her thoughts breaking through*) 'No, I'm not myself yet. That's just it. Not all myself. But I've been becoming myself. And I must finish.'" The action, the motivation, and the ideal development have all been made clear.

In the next act Nina has suffered the consequences of her revolt from her father's morality—her "destructive experiences" have resulted in total disillusion. But, meanwhile, she has been groping toward a new concept, or morality, which will give meaning to her life. And in a daring flight of imagination she suggests the outlines of her new mythical concept: "The mistake began when God was created in a male image. . . . The God of Gods—the Boss—has always been a man. That makes life so perverted, and death so unnatural. We should have imagined life as created in the birth-pain of God the Mother. Then we would understand why we, Her children, have inherited pain. . . ." In desperation Nina exclaims: "Oh God, Charlie, I want to believe in something!" But she has already suggested a new concept of the "Mother God" in which she can believe. And this myth, which is both created by and identified with the character of Nina, recalls the myth of the Old Testament God which gave meaning to the character of Ephraim Cabot in *Desire Under the Elms*. In each play, a kind of religious myth raises a seemingly realistic drama to new levels of meaning.

As the tortured plot of *Strange Interlude* unfolds, the actions and the words sometimes shock, sometimes strain the reader's credibility. After the heroine becomes "herself" again and marries, her mother-in-law reveals that there is insanity in the family. She tells a Gothic story of a madman in the attic, and asserts some facts of doubtful scientific truth about the hereditary nature of insanity. This is the weakest part of the play. But this melodrama is also part of the tradition of the Gothic and Romantic novel: the effect is psychological and mythical, rather than realistic. The complication of "insanity" which frustrates the normal life of the heroine forces her to seek self-realization through three men rather than one. And this develops both the element of dramatic tension which makes the play theatrically effective and that of myth which makes it significant.

The character of the heroine, Nina Leeds, is central. As the play develops she increases in stature until her realistic actions take on the quality of archetypal myth. As she struggles toward self-realization—in spite of the moral conventions of her Puritan past and in spite of the "insanity" of the world about her—her problems become those of "Everywoman." At the time that he was writing, O'Neill referred to it as "my woman play." And the strangely feminine quality of his insight becomes evident here: the play has always appealed with greatest force to women. Nina seems to embody the essence of "the eternal feminine"— what Goethe called "*das ewige weibliche.*" On the philosophical level her story realizes something of Schopenhauer's principle of "the will to live,"[5] and even suggests something of the old oriental myth of Maya, the goddess of illusion. In the character of Nina Leeds, O'Neill combined realistic characterization with mythical conception.

The skill with which the character of Nina Leeds is realized is attested by the theatrical and popular success of the play: beyond the creaky machinery of the plot, and the explicit psychology of the motivation, the central characters are realized by means of simple dialogue and spoken thoughts. Charlie Marsden, for instance, who both introduces and concludes the play, addresses Nina affectionately as "Nina, Cara Nina." And his casual pet name suggests the comparison of her character to Anna Karenina, at the same time that its literary self-consciousness helps to realize his own affected character. (O'Neill wrote: "It is his echo of 'Anna Karenina,' mixed with a flair for exhibiting a foreign language endearment. He is that sort, is Charlie."[6]) But most of all, the spoken thoughts of Nina Leeds carry conviction, and often raise the conscious psychology of the play to the level of intuitive truth. When Nina is tempted to tell her boyishly naïve husband that her baby is not actually his, she is suddenly prevented by her realization of his boyish trustfulness: "Nina (*thinking strangely*) 'Little boy! one gives birth to little boys! one doesn't drive them mad and kill them!" The very spontaneous simplicity of her intuitive feeling both startles and convinces. "Nina, Cara Nina," who has imagined God in the image of the Mother, becomes in dramatic concept the mother of illusion for her husband and her child, yet she remains dramatically real.

At the climax of the play, however, *Strange Interlude* goes beyond dramatic realism to act out one of the most strange but effective scenes in the modern theater. At the end of Act Six, Nina has just had a "healthy" baby by her lover to replace the one destroyed because of her husband's "insanity." As the baby sleeps in the next room, the husband, the lover, and the fatherly Charlie Marsden are gathered together. Nina "(*with a strange gaiety*)" exclaims: "Sit down, all of you! Make yourselves at home! You are my three men! This is your home with me!" And, in this increasingly unrealistic situation, the three men voice their unspoken thoughts, each revealing his imperfect understanding of their tangled relationship. After them, Nina thinks: "(*More and more strangely triumphant*) 'My three men! . . . I feel their desires converge in me! . . . to form one complete

beautiful male desire which I absorb . . . and am whole. . . .' "
And at the scene's end Nina kisses her husband *"as she might a
big brother,"* and Marsden *"as she might a father,"* but Darrell
"lovingly on the lips as she would kiss her lover." Considered
realistically the scene is incredible. Yet, in the theater, the
quality of subconscious realism triumphs over conscious reality,
and the interweaving of these twin realities produces a dramatic
myth not quite like anything else in literature.

Strange Interlude is a strange play. From its first performance
it has aroused conflicting emotions—of intense partisanship, and
of intense annoyance. It seems to some a great play; to others,
it seems merely pretentious. But beyond question it has been
successful. And it remains uniquely interesting.

III   Mourning Becomes Electra

In the central act of *Mourning Becomes Electra* (the seventh
of the thirteen acts of this trilogy), Orin Mannon explains how
he was wounded in the Civil War:

> . . . The next morning I was in the trenches. . . . I hadn't slept.
> My head was queer. I thought what a joke it would be on the
> stupid Generals like Father if everyone on both sides suddenly
> saw the joke war was on them and laughed and shook hands!
> So I began to laugh and walked toward their lines with my hand
> out. Of course, the joke was on me and I got this wound in the
> head for my pains. I went mad, wanted to kill, and ran on,
> yelling. . . .

Because his "head was queer," this modern hero attempted to
realize the ideal which Lazarus had earlier imagined. But
naturally Orin was wounded by the enemy, and reacted with
physical violence—and later with cynical disillusion. The incongruity between man's dream of peace and his practice of the
madness of war motivates the unrelieved violence and pessimism
of the drama.

This unrelieved violence, both physical and psychological, is
the most distinctive characteristic of *Mourning Becomes Electra*.
The structure of the Greek myth upon which it was patterned
required the physical violence, but the extreme of its disillusion
resulted more from the development of O'Neill's feeling and

thought. His new "Inferno" naturally complemented the "Paradiso" of *Lazarus*. But *Electra* became a total Inferno, both objective and subjective, unrelieved by heroism, or humor, or human warmth—unlike the original Greek tragedies, unlike Dante's *Inferno*, and indeed unlike O'Neill's own later drama of the lower depths, *The Iceman Cometh*. The logical perfection of *Electra*, and the sustained psychological intensity of its feeling, produced an artistic work of great power. But the absolute depravity which it dramatized made it seem melodramatic and sometimes incredible.

When the play was first produced, it was hailed with superlatives. Joseph Wood Krutch—who had earlier declared the incompatibility of "The Modern Temper" with true tragedy—compared it with "the very greatest works of dramatic literature." And no professional reviewer failed to be impressed by its stature and its theatrical power. Indeed, no other play by O'Neill, before or since, received such favorable first reviews. This play marked the high-water mark of his critical success. And O'Neill himself always believed this the best of his early plays.

Nevertheless, *Mourning Becomes Electra*, heralded as the greatest American tragedy, enjoyed only moderate success in the theater; it closed after a run of five months. And it has not been revived professionally in modern times. Although many have continued to praise it, others have felt that it lacked the illusion of reality. One who admires most of O'Neill's plays may yet believe that this one has been overpraised. Indeed, the very logical perfection of its artistic design may constitute its greatest fault. The heroes of this "Inferno" are neither noble, like Lazarus, nor even deeply human. The "mourning" which "becomes" this Electra is more formal than emotional. Because this Inferno is so absolute, its tragedy remains mostly one of the mind.

O'Neill planned *Electra* more carefully and more consciously than any other play: he worked on it longer, and he wrote and rewrote it oftener. And for the first time in his long career, he patterned a play upon classical mythology. In 1926 he noted his first suggestion for it: "Modern psychological drama using one of the old legend plots of Greek tragedy for its basic theme—the Electra story?—the Medea? Is it possible to get modern psychological approximation of the Greek sense of fate into such a play, which an intelligent audience of today, possessed of no belief in gods or supernatural retribution, could accept and be moved by?" Two years later, on the "Arabian Sea en route for China," he noted more suggestions for it. And five years later, in Paris, he finally noted: "All work finished——script off to the Guild." During the last three years, he had worked constantly on it, and had struggled heroically with its problems. No other project (except, of course, his long, and finally unfinished Cycle) caused him so much trouble. And the result was a triumph of conscious art. But the typical qualities of his most successful plays—imagination and insight—entered into this one only incidentally. In so far as he consciously worked with classical materials, he produced a neatly patterned drama; when he departed from classical myth, he communicated to this work more of the emotional urgency of his own feelings and imagination.

Mourning Becomes Electra is, of course, not one play but three, and is subtitled *A Trilogy.* Until shortly before its final production, O'Neill hoped to have the three plays produced on successive nights; but practical considerations prevailed, and the thirteen acts of the trilogy were produced together, following the marathon course of *Strange Interlude.* And this was both practical and artistic—the three plays had been planned and completed as a whole. Nevertheless, from its very first performance, many reviewers and readers have recognized that the third play differed from the first two. In the first two, O'Neill consciously translated classical myth into modern psychological terms; in the third, he created his own myth. The first two follow the Greek pattern more closely, whereas the third departs from it to describe a more modern "Electra." Whether one likes the first two plays best, because "O'Neill was never more fully an artist than in filling out this pattern to the limit of its possibilities as melodrama,"[1] or whether one prefers the "superb conclusion, completely his own," is a matter of taste.

Mourning Becomes Electra follows the pattern of the Greek trilogy in the essentials. The first play, entitled "The Homecoming," is closest to its original. It tells of the return of General Ezra Mannon (Agamemnon) from the Civil War, and of his murder by his wife, Christine (Clytemnestra), at the urging of her lover, Adam Brant (Aegistheus). And it ends with the

END of
1st Summary

confrontation of the mother by her daughter, Lavinia Mannon (Electra). Physically, the chief difference of the modern play from its original is that Christine and her lover do not stab the husband in his bath; she administers poison to him instead of the medicine he expects. But, if this difference of action seems minor, it points to a major difference of character. Neither Ezra nor Christine Mannon shares the heroic stature of the Greek Agamemnon and Clytemnestra. Ezra seems less the conquering hero than the lonely old man, and his guilt is disproportionally small—it is not the cruelty and self-willed pride of the Greek; it is only a puritanical failure to satisfy his wife in their love-relationship. And Christine shares neither the passionate hatred of Clytemnestra for her husband, nor her passionate love for Aegistheus. Rather she seems a neurotic, vindictive woman whose nature is poisonous rather than heroic. Although the first play explains the actions of the classical *Agamemnon* in modern psychological terms, it substitutes neurotic hatred for the full-blooded passion and violence of the original.

2nd Summary

The second play of the trilogy, entitled "The Hunted," also follows the essential outlines of its Greek original. It centers upon the character of Orestes—now Orin Mannon, who has just returned from the war as this play begins. Confronted with the proof of his mother's guilt, Orin hunts down her lover and shoots him. But he does not murder his mother, as in the original Greek. Instead he tells her of her lover's death and confronts her with her guilt and with his own confused hatred of it, so that she is driven to commit suicide. The substitution of this suicide for the murder of the Greek original again emphasizes the anti-heroic nature of the modern protagonists. Nevertheless, in the case of Orin (Orestes), "the furies" which were externalized in the Greek myth, now have been realized more dramatically in the tortured conscience of the modern "hero" and in the psychological confusions of his mind. And these psychological furies have been motivated more fully by the modern incident of Orin's mad laughter and wounding in the war. Therefore, Orin seems to be driven by the tortured conscience of all modern men, in their realization of the evil of world war.

3RD Summary

The third play of the trilogy, entitled "The Haunted" departs more radically (and purposefully) from the Greek originals. It centers upon the character of Electra rather than that of Orestes, and it ascribes to this new Electra the only heroism—and the only true tragedy—of the three plays. In the Greek, Electra had been married to a peasant farmer and had remained subordinate to her brother. But, in his earliest notes for the future plays, O'Neill directed: "Give modern Electra figure in play tragic ending worthy of character. In Greek story she peters out into undramatic married banality." And throughout the planning and writing of the trilogy he consistently developed this new conception, until "Electra" became the title figure.

Moreover, in changing the character of Electra from the Greek original, O'Neill also changed the action and the dramatic conception of the final play. Now, Orestes can no longer find absolution from the furies which drive him (as he does in the Greek); he accepts damnation for the evil of his nature, and commits suicide, concluding: "The damned don't cry!" But Electra triumphs over the evil of her heritage by recognizing it clearly, and by determining to live with it to the end: "I'm the last Mannon. I've got to punish myself." And she begins her penance by telling Hannah "to throw out all the flowers." She locks herself in with her memories: she will escape damnation by learning fully to understand her own past and how to "cry" or "mourn" for it. At the end the modern heroine regains her humanity by undertaking a tragedy greater than that of her ancestors. She, like her creator, begins her "long day's journey into night."

But the faults of the two earlier plays have lessened the effectiveness of this ending. The psychological motivation has been made too explicit. And although this motivation has seemed Freudian, it has exaggerated to the point of incredibility the fatal necessity of the Oedipus and Electra complexes. It has described the sinful love of the son for the mother and of the daughter for the father as a universal, compulsive pattern. These protagonists seem to have been born damned. Except for Electra, they do not achieve tragedy; they become merely the helpless victims of their inherited natures. And this psychological equivalent of original sin, which motivates the action of the play but destroys the conviction of its tragedy, is further explained intellectually by references to the New England puritanism of the Mannons. But clinical psychology and puritanism remain abstractions; they do not produce the dramatic illusion of reality.

O'Neill seems to have been aware of this difficulty, and he attempted to meet it by introducing a "chorus" of *"townsfolk . . . as a human background for the drama of the Mannons."* Contrasting with the inhuman Mannons, he introduced these "types," together with two individual "normal" characters, Peter and Hazel Niles. This brother and sister are described as in love with Lavinia and Orin Mannon, but they seem so innocent as to be unreal. They woodenly persist in their love for the Mannons, despite repeated rejections, insults, and desertions. And their total unreality (as contrasted with the reality of the innocent Sam Evans in *Strange Interlude*) makes the unrelieved depravity of the Mannons seem all the more incredible. A true Inferno must establish some dramatic relationship with the work-a-day world. But only Seth Beckwith, the caretaker for the Mannons, successfully relates them to the world of the living.

If abnormal psychology and the patterned puritanism of the modern Mannons make their Greek myth seem melodramatic and sometimes incredible, O'Neill did succeed in making it interesting, and, finally, tragic, by means of his own motivations and themes foreign to the Greek original. Most effective is the recurrent theme of the "Blessed Isles"—a dream of Eden which all the Mannons share, and which provides an internal contrast to the unrelieved evil of their psychology. The ancestral Mannons have actually sailed to the South Seas in their clipper ships. And Orin, who has read Melville's novels telling of his voyages to the Pacific, now dreams of going there himself. Christine and her lover are planning, when he is killed, to escape to the Blessed Isles by ship. And, finally, Lavinia and Orin do actually voyage there after the deaths of their parents. But (like Melville in actual fact) Orin rejects this ideal paradise to return to his puritan home. And Lavinia, who returns with him, realizes that her dream of escape has been only illusion and that she must face the ghosts of her past and accept her punishment for the evil of it. Thus the theme of the South Sea paradise recalls both the history and the literature of the American past, and it makes real the abstract pattern of the dramas, motivating the genuine tragedy of the conclusion.

But most strange is the combination of circumstance and symbol by which this formal trilogy seems to have dramatized the end of O'Neill's own tragic quest for "the secret hidden over there beyond the horizon." His first notes, describing his intention to give Electra the central role in the projected drama, were written on shipboard during his own voyage to the Orient and were datelined the "China Sea." Like his imagined Lavinia, he also had realized his dream of sailing to the East and, like her, had found only disillusion. And with Lavinia, he symbolically returned to his own land, renounced his dreams, and locked himself in with the ghosts of his family past. "I'll live alone with the dead, . . . and let them hound me, until the curse is paid out. . . . I know they will see to it I live for a long time." It would be ten long years before he could lay the ghosts and pay the curse by writing his *Long Day's Journey Into Night.*

CHAPTER 6

Days in the Wilderness

DURING ELEVEN YEARS from 1920 to 1931, O'Neill had written eleven major dramas and others of lesser importance. *Mourning Becomes Electra* marked the end of that era. All of these plays had been characterized by great originality and variety, but all had described in dramatic terms some aspect of his tragic quest for the "secret hidden over there beyond the horizon." He himself had sailed to the Orient while composing the last of these dramas, but he had found only disillusion. And *Mourning Becomes Electra* had described in dramatic terms this defeat.

There had been signs warning of this ending before *Mourning Becomes Electra*. In 1927, after finishing *Strange Interlude*, O'Neill had gone through a period of extreme emotional turmoil, during which he had ended his second marriage and had decided to marry his third wife, Carlotta Monterey. And the marital problems of these years certainly contributed to the confusion and failure of *Dynamo,* which had preceded *Mourning Becomes Electra,* both in writing and in production. Later he had explained that this play dated from a "time when I shouldn't have written anything." And, during his subsequent voyage to the Orient and the planning of *Mourning Becomes Electra,* his marital troubles continued to plague him. Undoubtedly these were related to the deeper spiritual restlessness which motivated the tragic questioning of all his plays, but both his marital and his spiritual problems came to a head at about this time.

About 1928, O'Neill entered a period of creation differing radically from the past. This period was characterized by uncertainty and spiritual "dryness." The powerful drive which had led to the outpouring of his major plays had now slackened. And this spiritual and creative drought caused the comparative failure of much of his work during the succeeding decade. It had left its mark even on *Mourning Becomes Electra,* and it determined the shifting patterns and moods of the ensuing plays. Those plays written during the 1930's which have survived (many were abandoned or destroyed) are all characterized by tentative beginnings and by a search for new patterns. They reflect the playwright's psychological and spiritual struggles in their subject matter, in their structure, and in their language.

Dynamo, for instance, was announced as the first play of a new "trilogy . . . that will dig at the roots of the sickness of today as I feel it. . . . The other two plays will be *Without Ending of Days,* and *It Cannot Be Mad.*" The second play of this "trilogy," which suffered many changes, finally emerged as *Days Without End.* The third was never written, and later its title (and perhaps even its identity) had changed in O'Neill's memory. In 1945 he wrote: "The only way to understand *Days Without End* is in its relationship to *Dynamo.* Originally these two plays were to be the first and second in a trilogy of 'God plays,' so to speak. Gold was to be the God of the third play. . . . The third play, 'The Career of Bessie Bowen' will never be written. The Great Depression caught up with its prophecies, for one thing."[1] Thus *Dynamo* and *Days Without End* were deliberately intended to dramatize O'Neill's search for a "God," or philosophy of life, adequate to a modern world suffering from "the sickness of today."

Days Without End described and sought to analyze this "sickness of today" more specifically. It explained that the sickness was caused by modern man's loss of faith which in turn was caused by his abandonment of past traditions and his heresy from orthodox religion. (Joseph Wood Krutch had described much the same thing earlier in *The Modern Temper.*) But the title of *Days Without End* also recalled another world-weariness of much the same kind described more eloquently by a tragedian four centuries before: "Tomorrow and tomorrow and tomorrow/Creeps in this petty pace from day to day. . . ." Although O'Neill's problem was no longer "To be or not to be," it remained essentially the same as Hamlet's: to absent himself from "felicity" while he made his peace with his father's ghost.

In the midst of his struggles to find a way out of the spiritual desert described in *Days Without End,* O'Neill reacted spontaneously by writing *Ah, Wilderness!* in four week's time. ("Only once before, in the case of *Desire Under the Elms,* has a plot idea come to me so easily. . . . I wrote it more easily than I have written any other of my works.") And he now luxuriated in the mood of sentimental comedy which the new play had dramatized. "I have a deep personal affection for that play," he wrote—"a feeling toward it that is quite apart from any consideration of it as a piece of dramatic writing by me as a playwright." He even expanded this feeling to cosmic proportions: "To me, the America which was (and is) the real America found expression in such middle-class families as the Millers."[2] Thus at the same time that he was analyzing the sickness of today and the spiritual desolation of the modern world, he was praising the sentimental goodness of that world and declaring that it constituted "the real America."

O'Neill's writing of *Ah, Wilderness!,* and his feeling of personal affection for the sentimental values of the play, seemed utterly to contradict his feeling of personal involvement with the spiritual desolation and world-weariness of the hero of *Days Without End.* But *Ah, Wilderness!* suggested the resolution of this seeming contradiction by its very title. Brooks Atkinson wrote that "in spite of its dreadful title, *Ah, Wilderness!* is a true and congenial comedy." But the title actually suggests the true meaning of the play. The spiritual "wilderness" of the modern world may seem like "paradise enow" if romantic love is all-sufficient. But the wilderness remains a wilderness for those who seek more deeply.

O'Neill was able to see the modern world from two opposite points of view at the same time. Moreover, he was able to dramatize these two mutually exclusive views of the world in two separate plays, written simultaneously. And most remarkable, he was able to identify himself emotionally with the two mutually exclusive sets of values of each play and to feel somehow that each represented "the true America." And yet he could suggest intellectually by the ambiguity of the title *Ah, Wilderness!* that both Americas were "real," that both sets of values could exist together.

The warm sentimentality of *Ah, Wilderness!* complemented perfectly the dry analysis of *Days Without End.* Referring to the latter play, O'Neill wrote:

> After all, this play, like *Ah Wilderness!* but in a much deeper
> sense, is the paying of an old debt on my part—a gesture toward
> more comprehensive, unembittered understanding and inner
> freedom—the breaking away from an old formula that I had
> enslaved myself with, and the appreciation that there is their own
> truth in other formulas, too, and that any life-giving formula
> is as fit a subject for drama as any other.[3]

Each of the plays attempted to discover a new "life-giving
formula." Each broke away from the "old formula that I had
enslaved myself with." But O'Neill still was seeking a "more
comprehensive, unembittered understanding and inner freedom,"
because each of these formulas remained exclusive. Only
gradually would he grope toward the comprehensive "formula,"
or dramatic philosophy, embodied in the final plays, which would
combine the values of the wilderness world with those of the
spirit. And this comprehensive formula would dramatize the
ambivalence which he felt toward "the real America," described
in mutually exclusive terms in *Days Without End* and *Ah,
Wilderness!*

Meanwhile, the idea of the wilderness itself seemed to offer
the possibility of reconciling these contradictions. Considered
in the context of American history, "wilderness" has implied
both the denial of traditional civilization and the opportunity
for building a new and better civilization. O'Neill's early plays
had idealized the wilderness of the sea and the jungle. The
end-papers of all his published plays had been decorated by
the design of a breaking wave. Now the new collected edition
of all his work issued in 1934 was entitled: *The Plays of Eugene
O'Neill: Wilderness Edition.*

Following the production—and failure—of *Days Without End,*
O'Neill decided to retire from the theater and to devote himself
to a new cycle of plays which would trace the rise and decline
of an Irish-American family through history. First announced
as a new trilogy, the "Cycle" gradually grew to include five plays,
then seven, then nine, and finally eleven. The title of the whole
also changed with the years: first *The Calms of Capricorn,* then
A Touch of the Poet, and finally *A Tale of Possessors Self-
Dispossessed.*[4] From 1935 to 1939 he devoted himself exclusively
to this project, but during these years he completed only the first

drafts of three of the eleven plays. He became progressively dissatisfied with the results, and in 1939 he set aside the work to write his final autobiographical plays. After completing these, his health made successful creation impossible; and, although he still worked on the plays of the Cycle, he gradually gave up hope for it. Finally he destroyed all the manuscripts of it except the single play, A Touch of the Poet, and (apparently by accident) the unfinished manuscript of More Stately Mansions.

The reason for his progressive dissatisfaction with the plays of the Cycle probably lay in his failure to discover any new "life-giving formula" to dramatize the successive tragedies of his Irish-American family through history. In a late interview he explained his interpretation of American history: "We've followed the same selfish greedy path as every other country in the world. We talk about the American Dream and want to tell the world about the American Dream, but what is that dream, in most cases, but the dream of material things. I sometimes think that the United States, for this reason, is the greatest failure the world has ever seen."[5] There is reason to believe that his Cycle became, progressively, a vehicle for his denunciation of the selfish materialism of American history and of what he considered the hypocrisy of "the American Dream."

In 1936 he wrote Lawrence Langner that he was concerned only with "the spiritual and psychological history of an American family in the plays. The Cycle is primarily that, the history of a family. What larger significance I can give my people as extraordinary examples and symbols in the drama of American possessiveness and materialism is something else again. But I don't want anyone to get the idea that this Cycle is much concerned with what is usually understood by American history, for it isn't."[6] But twelve years later in 1948, after informing Hamilton Basso that he had destroyed most of the manuscripts of the Cycle, he declared that it had been about "an American family primarily, but also intended to be the story of America." As "the story of America" the Cycle failed and was destroyed. But as "the history of a family in America," a portion of it survived and achieved success.

The key character in O'Neill's Cycle (in so far as we can judge by what has survived of it) was Deborah Harford, a New England aristocrat who appears in A Touch of the Poet (and also in the later play, *More Stately Mansions*) to confront her future daughter-in-law, Sara Melody. Her function in this play is largely expository, and her character is described as remote and ironic. Confronting Sara, she analyzes her son Simon's confused idealism, and traces it to its sources in history. This idealism derives from Simon's grandfather, who, because "he was a fanatic in the cause of pure freedom, became scornful of our Revolution." And it now expresses itself in the equally romantic dream of Simon, who "left home to seek self-emancipation at the breast of Nature." Deborah Harford, disbelieving in the American idealism which had inspired the Revolution and which now inspires her Transcendentalist son, explains to her future daughter-in-law how foolish it all is.

But the Irish Sara Melody hardly needs this ironic exposition by her New England mother-in-law of the falsity of Simon's American Dream; she has already explained it to her own mother in the beginning of the play:

> He's a born dreamer with a raft of great dreams, and he's very serious about them. . . . He wanted to prove his independence by living alone in the wilds, and build his own cabin, and do all the work, and support himself simply, and feel one with Nature, and think great thoughts about what life means, and write a book about how the world can be changed so people won't be greedy to own money and land and get the best of each other but will be content with little and live in peace and freedom together, and it will be like heaven on earth.
> *She laughs fondly—and a bit derisively.*

No character in *A Touch of the Poet* holds the slightest belief in the dreams of the American idealist, Simon Harford, who is described in almost exactly the same terms as the historic Henry David Thoreau. Neither this Transcendental dreamer, nor his Revolutionary ancestor is to be taken seriously. Rather he is to be regarded "fondly" and "derisively." O'Neill never allowed him to appear on the stage in *A Touch of the Poet,* and therefore he never seems real. All we know is that both his mother and his future wife agree in dismissing his dreams with amused contempt. O'Neill's utter disbelief in all American idealism, which he described as wholly romantic and therefore false, contributed to the failure of the projected Cycle. For the Cycle was based upon nineteenth-century American history. And all the historic American idealists enthusiastically believed in the American Dream.

A Touch of the Poet succeeded (while the other plays of the Cycle failed) because it was really two plays. The first part (which we have just described) was essentially expository, and it consisted of O'Neill's dry analysis of the idealism of early American history, which he considered to be at times hypocritical and always a possessive materialism in disguise. This was an interesting interpretation; but it was not true to history, and it was not dramatic. But the second part of the play resembled the subject matter of O'Neill's final autobiographical plays, and centered upon the Irish character of Cornelius Melody. And Melody—like James O'Neill and James Tyrone—had little to do with American history, except through the fact of his immigration. The bulk of *A Touch of the Poet,* which told his Irish story, proved both dramatic and successful. But it took O'Neill five years of thankless work and frustration to disentangle his own Irish family's autobiography from what he sometimes imagined to be "the story of America."

I Dynamo

Dynamo is probably the worst of the twenty "best" plays by O'Neill that we have chosen to consider individually. When first produced it was condemned by all the critics, and it ran for only fifty performances (enough to satisfy the Theatre Guild subscription list), even though it followed immediately the great popular success of *Strange Interlude.* Its plot seems contrived and its characters unreal. Yet, in spite of its dramatic failure and its literary inadequacy, it remains interesting as a play of ideas. And the dramatic image of the great dynamo, which dominates the final scenes, realizes a symbol of universal power.

The plot of *Dynamo* is neatly patterned, but the dialogue is melodramatic and the action strained to the point of incredibility. In the first act a fundamentalist minister and an atheistic engineer feud with each other. The minister's son loves the engineer's daughter, but his parents denounce the match. Then the son, Reuben Light, learns that his mother has betrayed his confidences to her. In revulsion he denounces both her and his father's God:

"If there is his God let him strike me dead this second. I dare him!"

(*His father squeals with terror. . . . His mother screams. He laughs triumphantly.*)

"There! Didn't I tell you! . . . There is no God. No God but Electricity. I'll never be scared again!"

In the second act Reuben, several years older, returns home to learn that his mother has died of grief. He feels remorse for her, but he has become cynical about love, and he deliberately seduces the engineer's daughter. He gets a job in the power plant and confronts the dynamo, which he worships as the source and symbol of all power: "'a great dark mother! that's what she is!' (*He gets down on his knees and prays aloud to the dynamo.*) 'Oh, Mother of Life, my mother is dead . . . tell her to forgive me, and to help me find your truth.'" Then he thinks to himself: "Yes, that did it. . . . I feel I'm forgiven."

In the third act the hero is torn between lust for the engineer's daughter and worship of the dynamo, which (apparently) has now taken on the attributes of his father's God. "I was living in sin," he muses, "——Dynamo would never find me worthy of her secret until I'd given up the flesh and purified myself." Hoping to make the engineer's daughter worship the dynamo with him, he drags her to the power house; but, feeling only lust, he shoots her, and then immolates himself by throwing his body across the dynamo: "(*there is a flash of bluish light about him, and all the plants dim down.*)" When he has died, the engineer's wife pounds on the dynamo and "(*in a fit of childish anger*)" exclaims: "You hateful old thing, you!"—— *Curtain!*

It is hard to take all this seriously. The characters are not people, but puppets. The minister "squeals with terror." The son shoots his sweetheart just because she will not worship his "Dynamo." The girl's mother is a caricature of the "earth-mother" she is supposed to suggest. And the hero Reuben is a "rube." The human characters and their actions are not believable. But the true hero of *Dynamo*, as the title suggests, is not a human being, but a machine. And *Dynamo* derives its genuine symbolic power from a combination of challenging ideas, of personal experience, and of imaginative symbolism.

A generation earlier in the Paris exposition of 1900, Henry Adams, who had stood in the hall of science, had felt "the forty foot dynamos as a moral force, much as the early Christians felt the Cross." In his classic *Autobiography,* he had devoted his most striking chapter to "The Dynamo and the Virgin." Now O'Neill attempted to dramatize this religious idea. And, although the dramatization was not successful, he did develop the idea effectively. His dynamo now suggested—not the religious power of the Christian Virgin—but rather the universal power of the "dark mother." And his plot—unreal as it was—suggested that this new religion of the dynamo was a worship of mechanical power divorced from purpose, and of biological sex divorced from love—of a pagan "dark mother" who destroyed even her own children.

The best part of *Dynamo* consists of the realistic but also symbolic stage directions for the giant dynamo. O'Neill himself had visited a power plant in Connecticut several years earlier, and had been impressed by the same sensuous realization of the idea of power in the low, continuous humming of the dynamo which had earlier impressed Henry Adams. When the play was to be produced, he wrote urging the stage designer to visit a power plant himself, to experience the actual impression which he wished reproduced. Lee Simonson has recorded how carefully he followed these directions, and how he was impressed by the accuracy of O'Neill's observations.[7]

But beyond realism, O'Neill went on to suggest the symbolic intention of the image of the dynamo upon the stage. The dynamo first appears, "*huge and black, with something of the massive female idol about it, the exciter set on the main structure like a head with blank, oblong eyes above a gross, rounded torso.*" And later from another angle, the dynamo is seen with its "*oil switches, their six cupped arms stretching upward, like queer Hindu idols tortured into scientific supplications.*" The great mother of religious mythology is partially realized in the dramatic description of the dynamo, even though the drama itself fails.

[*142*]

II Days Without End

Days Without End, almost as poor a play as *Dynamo,* remains much more interesting. It failed on the stage, yet it appealed to many readers and critics sympathetic to its predominantly Catholic point of view. The play was tried out in Boston—a strongly Catholic city—and received some favorable reviews. And in New York a minority praised it. Clearly it described the hero's quest for a true faith in the modern world, and clearly its story was autobiographical. O'Neill himself was going through a crisis at the time, and the play seems to reveal him wrestling with his conscience and thinking out loud. Moreover, this was the second of his projected "trilogy" of "God plays," and the second of his attempts to probe "the sickness of today." If the structure of the play was uncertain and the ending unconvincing, the fault lay partly in the nature of the subject and of the author's approach to it.

The action of the play is almost entirely psychological. The hero, John Loving, appears on the stage as two different people. The first is "John," a healthy, ingenuous extrovert; the second is "Loving," a cynical, embittered introvert. The opposing selves are played by different actors: "John" is unmasked, but "Loving" wears "the death mask of a JOHN who has died with a sneer of scornful mockery on his lips." The other important characters are John's wife and a Catholic priest who is also John's uncle. The drama, of course, centers on the struggle for the soul of "John Loving." Will the good John return to the true faith, proclaimed by his uncle the priest? Or will his mephistophelian alter ego, who preaches the modern religion of scientific rationalism, triumph?

The chief fault of the play is suggested by the terms in which the two opposing selves of the hero are described. The one is wholly kind and good; the other, wholly malicious and bad. In designing the play, O'Neill clearly weighted the scales against the modern, rationalistic self, "Loving." The author's emotional involvement with his characters and the language which he put into their mouths made it necessary for him to conclude the play with the triumph of "John" over "Loving"—of good over evil. But the remarkable fact is that, despite his conscious weighting of the scales against one character and against one half of himself, he nevertheless could never convince either himself, or his audience, that this "good" ending was either true of just. He struggled through more different drafts of the play than for any earlier work, and with each draft he changed either the motivation or the ending. And the final form represented—as he admitted to a friend—a kind of "wish-fulfillment" on his part.

Days Without End, therefore, was both too abstract and too explicit for successful theater. Yet the plot succeeded in suggesting with remarkable accuracy the story of its author's spiritual struggle. "John" is writing a novel narrating the hero's unfaithfulness to his wife. But he cannot decide how to end it: will the wife forgive him, because he genuinely repents his infidelity? Or will she despair and die, because he genuinely desires her death? He cannot decide, so he outlines the plot to his wife and his uncle. And she, of course, recognizes it as the true story of their relationship. She runs out into a storm and contracts pneumonia. Will she live, and will "John" be saved? Or will she die, and will "Loving" be damned?

The successive manuscript outlines and drafts of the play have been preserved in the O'Neill collection in Yale University Library, and they have been described clearly by Doris Falk.[8] In the first version of the play, the hero himself commits suicide because he recognizes the evil of his own nature. In the second, O'Neill changed the hero's motivation to make him recognize that his own evil is really the original sin of Man, for whose punishment Christ has already endured crucifixion. In the third, he went to the other extreme of nihilistic tragedy; he made the hero's wife die, while the hero ended cursing God. In the fourth, he made the hero recognize his fault, but only at the very moment of his death. In the fifth, he changed this to make the hero's rational self recognize the illogic of his own apostasy: "But if I curse, I must [also] believe!" In the sixth version he moved to the final, official ending of the play, in which the hero proclaims his victory over disbelief, and all ends well. But still O'Neill's dissatisfaction showed itself in several minor changes and revisions with which he attempted to modify this officially happy ending.

The publication and production of *Days Without End* caused a controversy among the playwright's admirers. His Catholic friends hailed it as a manifesto of his own victory over despair.

But his agnostic friends denounced it as an apostasy from his life-long quest for objective truth. Benjamin de Casseres exclaimed that "O'Neill had betrayed his Demon," and wrote a violent parody of the play. But Richard Skinner interpreted the play as the climax of a long series in which the author had sought to describe his own quest for faith in the modern world, and he went on to write a book to illustrate this, entitled: *Eugene O'Neill: A Poet's Quest.* Meanwhile O'Neill himself remained aloof. But years later, when asked if he had truly returned to the Catholic faith, he replied: "Unfortunately, no."

But, if the play did not describe the playwright's own escape from the wilderness of disbelief, it did mark a milestone in his quest for some "more comprehensive, life-giving formula." Technically, the plot suggested a kind of alternative-choice formula, which establishes an almost exact correspondence between the author's actual search for an ideal "ending" and the struggles of his hero in the play. For practical purposes, of course, this plot required that the author choose one ending to the exclusion of all other possible ones. Ideally, however, the "life-giving formula" toward which O'Neill was groping would not require the final choice of one "faith," or ending, to the exclusion of others. It would accept uncertainty, or multiplicity of choice, as the essence of its drama; and it would not weight the scales in favor of any one character or faith. But before discovering this ideal "formula," O'Neill would experiment with others.

III   Ah, Wilderness!

Ah, Wilderness! is the only comedy among O'Neill's major works. And, after writing the play, which (he recognized) "is so out of my previous line," he confessed himself uncertain about its quality. But others, including producers, critics, audiences, and readers, have enthusiastically welcomed the play from the beginning. And its success suggests that O'Neill could have written many conventional comedies of the kind if he had wished. But he did not, partly because it was "out of my line," technically, but more important because this play was outside his experience, autobiographically. It described (as he was careful to emphasize) the happy boyhood and adolescence which he might have had, but which the tragic background of his family's life had made impossible.

The play is, therefore, partly a comedy of wish fulfillment. "That's the way I would have liked my boyhood to have been," he said. But it is partly, also, a comedy of observation. His biographers have identified many of its characters with the friends and acquaintances of his New London youth. The difference between *Ah, Wilderness!* and other sentimental comedies of family life set at the turn of the century is that, although it describes that life somewhat sentimentally, it also suggests the dark side of the picture. Apparently it dramatizes the problems of American adolescence with all the cheerful superficiality of Booth Tarkington's *Seventeen*. But it also suggests the dark underworld of alcoholism, prostitution, and spiritual despair and it does so with something of the inwardness of J. D. Salinger's *Catcher in the Rye*. All the usual humorous and even ridiculous problems of adolescence appear; and, of course, the play ends happily. But it does not suggest—as Booth Tarkington's novels do—that these are the problems of adolescence only and that they will always be solved happily by the mere process of time.

All the characters of the play (except for the briefly malevolent father of Muriel) are good people. Nat Miller, the father of the young hero, is described as "too decent for your own good." His son, Richard, although tempted by all the "immoral" literature and life which had so influenced O'Neill himself, is basically innocent and utterly truthful. The alcoholic uncle, obviously modeled on Eugene's brother, Jamie, nevertheless recognizes his own fault; and, unlike Jamie, he does everything he can to prevent the corruption of his nephew. When young Richard comes home drunk, it is Uncle Sid who takes him in charge: "Come on, Old Sport! Upstairs we go! Your old Uncle Sid will fix you up. He's the kid that wrote the book!" It is as if the man who wrote the play were also watching over his characters to see that they did not follow his own dangerous path.

Yet, *Ah, Wilderness!* is never merely sentimental comedy. It is always ironic, and this irony gives a biting edge to its humor, especially when it seems in danger of becoming too bland. The values of conventional middle-class morality remain dominant, but they are seldom described as ideal. The Miller's house, for example, is *"furnished with scrupulous medium-priced taste-lessness of the period"* and the *"walls are papered with a cheer-ful, ugly blue design."* Neither the helpless innocence of the hero's mother nor even the fumbling goodness of his father is idealized. Instead, their values are dramatized, much as O'Neill himself described them, as a kind of "life-giving formula." Their goodness is not final but conditional. And young Richard's brief revolt against these values becomes, therefore, also reasonable. When drunk, *"he laughs with a double-dyed sardonicism."* He sees the absurdity of the conventional values, but his author also sees the absurdity of his wholesale revolt. Although the values of the play are "life-giving," their seeming positiveness is the result of a double negative. If *Ah, Wilderness!* dramatized a nostalgic "paradise" which O'Neill never knew, its backdrop (both physical and spiritual) is still the "wilderness."

IV A Touch of the Poet

"There will be nothing of *Ah, Wilderness!* or *Days Without End* in this Cycle," O'Neill wrote in 1937; "they were an inter-lude." And he reported progress: "one play in good shape, need-ing only revising."[9] But *A Touch of the Poet,* the first play of the Cycle to be written, proved to need so much "revising" that it was never released in his lifetime. While working on his final autobiographical plays about 1942, he rewrote it. And in 1947 he tentatively released it for production, along with *A Moon for the Misbegotten.* But he withdrew it in discouragement when the latter play failed and was withdrawn. After his death it was finally published in 1957, and was produced on Broadway a year later. More than twenty years had intervened between its first writing and its final production.

A Touch of the Poet belongs to two different periods of composition and to a third of theatrical production. It is partly an exemplar of his historic Cycle that failed; but it is partly related, also, to his three final autobiographical plays: he described it in a later announcement as making a fourth with this trilogy. Finally, when the play was published and produced, critics and readers were unable to make up their minds about it. Perhaps it should be considered the last of all O'Neill's major plays. But much of its theme and its technique mark it, rather, as the last of O'Neill's "wilderness" plays.

When *A Touch of the Poet* was finally produced, it was received with mixed praise. Some of O'Neill's admirers disliked it, others praised the play; and the theater-going public welcomed its rich Irish humor. Perhaps the most perceptive criticism was that of Henry Hewes: "European romance mixes with American materialism," he wrote; but "O'Neill never shows much of the Yankee side of the picture." The play "suffers somewhat from over-exposition, too many vital scenes occurring offstage." Yet "it foreshadows O'Neill's growth into his final great period."[10]

The plot of this play is so complex and so skillfully constructed that it moves to its tragi-comic conclusion with great theatrical success. Only a second reading and careful analysis suggest that it really consists of two separate plots. In the first, all the action occurs offstage, while the story and motivation are explained by Sara Melody and by Deborah Harford. It tells of the seduction of Simon Harford, the American dreamer, by Sara Melody, the Irish realist. And in this action the Irish daughter Sara and the American mother Deborah seem almost to cooperate in their joint effort to wean the idealistic Simon away from all his foolish idealism. He has been trying to live the simple life "at the breast of nature," "thinking great thoughts" and writing poetry; but he has become sick and is being nursed back to health by Sara. His mother Deborah now visits Sara, ostensibly to warn her not to try to seduce Simon into marriage. But Deborah can only philosophize, and she ends by declaring that "I shall never venture forth again to do my duty." Her departure (at the end of Act Two) leaves Sara in possession of the field, and her future conquest of Simon becomes a foregone conclusion. This plot, obviously the original one, is central to the great Cycle, and describes the origin of O'Neill's fictional "Irish-American family" in history.

But the second plot, which is built around the first, is more colorful, more convincing, and much more dramatic. It tells of the conflict between the realistic Sara Melody and her romantic Irish father, Cornelius. "Con" Melody, who had been a major in Wellington's army, now imagines himself to be a great gentleman who is far above the "common" people with whom he is forced to associate. His romantic dreams of grandeur obviously lack foundation either in the European past or in the American present, and his daughter struggles to force him to recognize the truth about himself. At the end she succeeds, and her father, with his romantic dreams destroyed, retires to his whiskey.

Sara Melody, the determined realist, is left in possession of the field at the end of the play, as she had been at the end of the first two acts. She has achieved victory, first, over the American idealism of her future husband and, finally, over the Irish romanticism of her old father. Presumably, she will convert her husband to her own realistic point of view, and they will build "more stately mansions" in the new America. But will this be realism, or materialism? In terms of American history, Sara's seduction of her husband, and the consequent destruction of his idealism, is materialistic. But her victory over her father, and the consequent destruction of his romantic delusion, is realistic.

The second part of *A Touch of the Poet*, which describes the humiliation of Major Cornelius Melody and his romantic Irish pride, represents O'Neill at his best. Although really the son of an Irish peasant, Melody—an immigrant to New England and keeper of a run-down tavern in a small town—pretends to be a fine gentleman and military hero, and constantly recites Byron and exaggerates the stories of his past exploits. And this might all seem harmless enough. But he also treats his wife like a servant, browbeats his daughter, tries to seduce the aristocratic Deborah Harford, and then rushes off to challenge her husband to a duel. After a magnificent donnybrook, he is subdued by the local police and returns to his tavern a beaten man. In final recognition of his defeat, he goes out to the stable, where he keeps the beautiful mare which he treasures as the evidence and the symbol of his aristocratic pretensions, and shoots her.

The excellence of the second half of the play lies in the perfect balance between its conflicting characters and motives. Cornelius Melody is always a sympathetic character, because, like most of O'Neill's heroes, he is torn by conflicting inner forces. He acts out a "role that has become more real than his real self to him." But he is also the aggressive egotist, whose delusions of grandeur cannot be tolerated and accepted—like those of the drunken bums in *The Iceman Cometh*—because they are dangerous. And con-

versely, his daughter Sara often seems an unsympathetic character, although she is obviously right in opposing his play-acting
and his tyranny. Like Hickey in *The Iceman,* she herself seems
the tyrant when she seeks to destroy his romantic delusions. But
unlike Hickey, she is wholly sane; therefore, her final victory
over her deluded father becomes both necessary and tragic. And
she ends by recognizing and accepting the tragedy of her own
victory: "But why should I cry, Mother? Why do I mourn for
him?" In the perfect balance and tragic transcendence of the
emotions dramatized, the second part of this play belongs to
"O'Neill's final great period."

CHAPTER 7

The Final Plays:
Journey Beyond Night

IN 1939 O'Neill abandoned work on the Cycle, on which he had been laboring for five years, and turned to a group of autobiographical plays, which he had been contemplating for much longer than that. As early as 1928 he had projected: "the grand opus of my life—the autobiographical *Sea-Mother's Son*"; and now, warned by physical illness that time might be running short, he turned to this final project. In six brief months he wrote the over-length play, *The Iceman Cometh*; and in the next three years completed *Long Day's Journey Into Night* and *A Moon for the Misbegotten.*

The action of these final plays takes place in the year 1912—the crucial one of O'Neill's life, which ended with his commitment to a tuberculosis sanitarium. All three are "autobiographical" in that they deal with characters and events roughly corresponding to those of his own family and life. But only *Long Day's Journey* is strictly autobiographical, and (as we have seen in Chapter One) even it diverged widely from the factual truth. In *The Iceman* no character related to the author appeared at all; and in *A Moon*, only one character (based on his brother Jamie). Although these plays were vaguely autobiographical, their distinctive quality was not due to their subjects but to their psychological meaning and to their dramatic technique.

It is too soon to speak of these late plays with assurance, but their nature is gradually becoming clear. They seem to dramatize the factual material of autobiography, but their exact meaning and even the motivation of their characters often remain ambiguous—and will probably always remain so. They dramatize a new technique of ambiguity, and they suggest a new meaning of equivalence.

All these final plays combine low comedy with high tragedy. O'Neill called it "a big kind of comedy that doesn't stay funny very long." When *The Iceman* was first produced, he criticized the cast for playing it as tragedy too soon. *Long Day's Journey* also begins with the burlesque story of Shaughnessy's pigs. And *A Moon* alternates between pigsty comedy and serious tragedy almost to the end. There is no clear distinction of genre in these plays—neither director nor reader can be sure just how they should be acted or understood.

More fundamental than this ambiguity of genre, or mood, however, is the deeper ambiguity of character, or motivation. Although each major character is realized in action and in speech, his inner nature is never finally determined. The first production of *The Iceman,* for instance, portrayed Hickey as a well-meaning man, driven to desperation by his own sinful nature and by his wife's excessive meekness. But the second production of the play triumphed over the first, largely because Hickey now became a kind of deluded messianic enthusiast, preaching his own confusion in the name of truth. But since O'Neill helped direct the first production, and not the second, it seems that even he did not know exactly how Hickey's motives should be defined. The "truth" about him was—and still remains —ambiguous.

In all the early plays O'Neill described the "quest" of his heroes for some "secret" of life "hidden over there beyond the horizon." The tragedies dramatized the sufferings of their heroes, and told how these often led to a tragic recognition of their nature, and sometimes to a transcendence of it. *Mourning Becomes Electra* ended with the heroine's final recognition of her evil nature, and *Lazarus Laughed* described the hero's final transcendence, in eloquent terms.

But in these final plays the tragic hero is no longer the active seeker, nor does he achieve the tragic "recognition" or the personal "transcendence" of the early plays. He seems instead the bemused spectator of the tragedy, and his "transcendence" is, at best, the recognition that there is no final "secret" to be discovered. Instead of exotic quests through alien lands by an "Emperor" Jones, or a "Marco Millions," the hero explores his own past and finally confronts himself. In this sense these plays are autobiographical. But they do not dramatize explicitly any tragic "recognition" by the hero: this is achieved, rather, by the author—and through him by the audience. And it is incorporated into the structure of the play. These final dramas no longer describe the tragic transcendence—they practice it.

I The Iceman Cometh

When *The Iceman Cometh* was produced by the Theatre Guild in 1946, the critics and the public received it with mixed reactions. A few called it O'Neill's best; others thought it a monumental bore; all felt it was much too long. Many were depressed by its unrelieved pessimism, and the public mood of post-World-War II exhaustion proved generally unfavorable to it. But several critics who then condemned it later changed their opinions radically. In 1956 a new production of the play sharpened its focus, a more cheerful public welcomed its tragic emotions, and a re-reading and thoughtful reconsideration made clear its depth and scope. In the eighteen years since its first production more perhaps has been written about this drama than about any other in a comparable period. Many still call it O'Neill's best, and all have been fascinated by its combination of deep feeling and artistic complexity. This play, which exists on many levels, can be seen and read many times without exhausting its possibilities.

On the realistic level, the play describes a group of drunken bums who inhabit Harry Hope's saloon in lower New York—"a cheap ginmill" modeled closely on "the Hell-Hole" and "Jimmy-the-Priest's" of O'Neill's own beachcombing days. Many of the characters have been identified with his actual friends of that time:[1] "Jimmy Tomorrow," the gentle dreamer, with James Findlater Byth; "Hugo Kalman," the anarchist, with Hippolyte Havel, an actual friend of the famous Emma Goldman; and "Larry Slade," the disillusioned philosopher, with O'Neill's own mentor, Terry Carlin. The play, therefore, is "autobiographical" in setting, in characterization, and, finally, in "philosophy." "The philosophy," O'Neill explained to an interviewer, "is that there is always one dream left, one final dream, no matter how low you have fallen, down there at the bottom of the bottle. I know, because I saw it."

But on the allegorical level, the play dramatizes a group of moral abstractions. The name of Harry "Hope" is obvious. And his saloon is succinctly characterized early in the play: "It's the No Chance Saloon. It's Bedrock Bar, The End of the Line Cafe, The Bottom of the Sea Rathskeller!" In this "Lower Depths" Harry Hope serves the alcohol which nourishes the "pipe dreams" of these pitiful people until "the iceman" (Death) finally "cometh." All this allegory seemed so obvious, indeed, that some early critics thought the play contrived and lacking in "reality."

But on a third level the play is neither concrete autobiography nor abstract allegory; it is a modern myth. And to this myth the character of Hickey, the hardware salesman, is central. He is fully realized in concrete detail and action, although he corresponds to no actual person among O'Neill's acquaintances. He is, rather, the archetypal American salesman, resembling in some ways Arthur Miller's Willie Loman and in others O'Neill's own Marco Millions. Yet he is a unique creation, and his true nature— as gradually revealed by the dialogue and action—is the true subject of the play.

The plot of *The Iceman* is built around the annual visit of Hickey to Harry Hope's saloon on the proprietor's birthday. In the past Hickey had regularly come to initiate a monumental drunken party, and the denizens all idolize his hearty good fellowship. But this year he tells them that he has reformed, and he tries to "sell" them his new brand of "salvation." He wheedles and argues to persuade them to give up their alcoholic "pipe dreams" and to face reality by venturing forth from the saloon into the outside world. They do so reluctantly, but (as could have been predicted) they soon return in despair and seek to drown their sorrows again in drink. But now the alcohol seems to have lost its power.

This simple plot occupies the first three and a half acts, which take about three and a half hours to play. No wonder some of the first audiences found the drama slow, sometimes tedious. But gradually it becomes clear that this plot is actually not the important one. The true plot of *The Iceman* is not realistic but psychological, for it consists not in the physical action, but in the gradual revelation of the motives for Hickey's sudden reformation and for his attempt to reform all his drunken friends. Why has this jovial American salesman of hardware suddenly become a fanatical, messianic salesman of salvation? Why is he trying to destroy the harmless pipe dreams of his alcoholic friends and to force them to face "reality"?

On the realistic level, of course, this seems to be no problem at all. Civilized society has always condemned alcoholism and has always sought to make its citizens face "reality." Therefore, Hickey seems merely the voice of civilized society—the reformed alcoholic who has finally faced the truth.

But, from the beginning of the play, Harry Hope and his alcoholic friends have felt that there was something wrong with the new Hickey. They know that in the past he has always returned home from his drunken binges to a long-suffering wife who has loved him so much that she has always forgiven him his infidelities. And he himself has always joked about her faithfulness, hinting that she, in turn, must have been having an affair with "the iceman" while he has been away. But now it gradually becomes clear that something has happened to Hickey's wife. Larry Slade, the philosopher, senses this and taunts Hickey: "Did this great revelation . . . come to you after you found that your wife was sick of you?" And at the end of the second act Hickey admits that he has pulled "that iceman gag" once too often: "I'm sorry to tell you that my dearly beloved wife is dead." All his friends are shocked, and feel sorry for him: Hickey must have reformed because of his sorrow and his shame at his shabby treatment of his dead wife. And throughout the next act this impression continues, only to be intensified at the end of the third act when Hickey lets it be known that "My poor wife was killed." But why?

The fourth (and last) act of the play is devoted to answering this question. In what has been called the longest soliloquy ever delivered on the New York stage, Hickey tries to explain why he has just killed his wife—"Only I've got to start way back at the beginning or you wouldn't understand." His long confession seeks to justify the motives of his twisted mind. But his friends only react in shocked disbelief: "You mad fool!" As he goes on, two detectives enter to apprehend him for the murder, but they also stand listening to his confession in fascination. He says that he killed his wife "to give her peace," so that she wouldn't have to suffer any more from her pipe dream that he would "behave." But at the climax of his confession, he suddenly blurts out his unconscious hatred for her; and then he immediately realizes that, if this is true, "I must have been insane." And his friends quickly fasten upon this answer, not only because it offers the only rational explanation of his actions, but also because it frees them of the responsibility of taking his earlier moral preachings seriously. They can now return happily to their liquor and their pipe dreams: "Bejees, fellers, I'm feeling the old kick." Meanwhile the detectives lead Hickey away to prison, where, they suppose, "he'll plead insanity."

Realistically, this long confession is a masterpiece of exposition of abnormal psychology. But its true function is not expository, but dramatic. The effect of Hickey's self-revelation is to unsettle all the old certainties and moral judgments which the realism of the first three acts has seemed to establish. If Hickey, who had seemed the voice of reason and social morality, was insane, then the drunken derelicts of Harry Hope's saloon were justified in resisting his attempts to reform them. Not their pipe dreams but his assumptions of moral superiority were false. And, with this, all the old truisms of morality and philosophy seem suddenly to crumble. And the "half-drunken mockery," which Larry Slade enunciated at the very beginning of the play, becomes a sober warning, reaffirmed at the end: "To hell with the truth! As the history of the world proves, the truth has no bearing on anything. It's irrelevant and immaterial, as the lawyers say. The lie of a pipe dream is what gives life to the whole misbegotten mad lot of us, drunk or sober."

This sudden revelation of the ambivalence of human motives and of the ambiguity of "truth" itself—coming as it does at the end of the play—bursts like a bomb in the mind. The last act of *The Iceman* demands a revaluation of all the earlier action. It shocks, but it also illuminates, and sends the audience home in a bemused trance. What is the truth about Hickey and his drunken friends? And what—for that matter—is Truth itself? Are men's dreams the only realities? "We are such stuff as dreams are made on." But then nirvana, or the recognition that all life is illusion, becomes the final goal of life. And man's recognition that he can never know "the secret" becomes the ultimate wisdom.

This philosophy, which is explicitly stated and implicitly suggested by the play, is deeply pessimistic. It has also been described as morbid, unhealthy, and fatalistic—the product of O'Neill's own "spiritual trauma." It has been said to summarize the message of all his dramas: "dream, drunkenness, and death" are the ends of life.[2] And this philosophy, it has been argued, results in "paralysis" and in a "fatal balance" in which all values cancel each other out. It dramatizes "the existential dilemma," "the problem of projecting value in a world devoid of absolutes," and "that terrifying freedom from which most of us feel compelled to escape."[3]

It is true that the philosophy of *The Iceman* is pessimistic. But it is not true (I believe) that it is morbid, unhealthy, or even fatalistic. Rather the opposite. It implies that pipe dreams and drunkenness *may* be more sane and more life-giving than moral self-righteousness. But it never idealizes dream or drunkenness, nor does it sentimentalize the drunken bums of Harry Hope's saloon. These represent humanity in its lowest depths. But, perhaps because the dreams of these men are so pitiful, they seem all the more human. And "there's something not human" about the moralistic Hickey, who tries to kill men's dreams. *The Iceman* becomes O'Neill's testament to humanity at its lowest.

The play has often been compared to Gorky's *The Lower Depths*,[4] but an excellent analysis of the two by Helen Muchnic points to their significant differences. Gorky's hero prophesies the ideal of social action by which a materialistic society may ultimately raise men from these lower depths. But O'Neill's play denies the ultimate value of all social action, for it idealizes man's understanding and compassion for his fellow man. *The Iceman* gives highest expression to O'Neill's lifelong belief that emotion is more important than action. On the practical level, therefore, the play and its philosophy are pessimistic. But, in its dramatic realization that human beings even at their lowest may understand and feel compassion for one another, it is optimistic.

O'Neill's "pessimism" is emphasized repeatedly by the dramatic character of Larry Slade, the philosopher. Therefore many critics have tried to identify Larry with O'Neill himself. And if Larry *is* O'Neill, then the message of *The Iceman* is despair. But the stage directions for Larry suggest association not with

O'Neill but with his early mentor, Terry Carlin. And Larry's exasperated condemnation of Don Parritt, at the end of the play, represents his dramatic failure to practice the philosophy he preaches. O'Neill himself stood apart from Larry, and from all the characters whom he had created in this play and in all his final ones. He dramatized his philosophy—and its failures—in action. And he realized the ideal of compassionate understanding and feeling by means of the myth, which gives form and meaning to the play.

II Long Day's Journey Into Night

Chapter One has already described the autobiographical aspects of *Long Day's Journey*: the conflict of autobiographical fact with artistic fiction in "The Start of the Journey," and the pervasive theme of homelessness which makes the play "An American Tragedy." This chapter will discuss the play as an original work of art and its relationship to O'Neill's other works.

Long Day's Journey marks the climax of O'Neill's development, both psychological and artistic. From the beginning of his career he had attempted to transmute his autobiographical experiences into art: *Exorcism, The Straw,* and *Welded* had all described the artist as hero; but all had failed, either because of sentimentality or because of idealization. In 1928 he had consciously projected an autobiographical work as his "grand opus." And now, twelve years later, he realized this lifelong ambition with the writing of *Long Day's Journey*. During these years he had effectively purged himself of his former pride and self-pity. And on completing the play, he recognized it, objectively, as his masterpiece.

After writing *Long Day's Journey*, O'Neill stipulated that it should not be produced until twenty-five years after his death. But in 1950, after the death of Eugene, Jr., he relented somewhat, and in 1956 his widow approved its publication and production. The Royal Dramatic Theatre of Stockholm was awarded first rights because O'Neill had been impressed by earlier Swedish productions of his plays and had been disappointed by the American reception of *The Iceman* and *A Moon*. But *Long Day's Journey* achieved immediate critical praise and popular success with both the Swedish and the American productions. Although some critics complained of its length and its unrelieved pessimism, the majority was enthusiastic. And many, who had formerly disliked O'Neill, admired this play. Stephen Whicher witnessed its Swedish premiere, and, although "starting with a prejudice against O'Neill,"[5] was impressed both by the play and by the fascinated attention of the audience throughout its four and a half hours on the stage. In America most serious critics were enthusiastic. And T. S. Eliot gave testimony to an enthusiasm which he had not felt for the earlier dramas of the author. Since then the play's reputation has steadily increased. And the moving picture version, which follows the text closely, achieved further success.

The reasons for the excellence of *Long Day's Journey* are not immediately apparent. Its style approximates Edmund Tyrone's description: "It will be faithful realism, at least." But the realism achieves a transcendence unequaled in the earlier dramas, and it is "faithful" not to the letter but to the spirit of its auto-biographical materials. The story of Edmund Tyrone and his family is essentially the story of the young O'Neill. But the illumination which flashes through it, like the beams from the lighthouse through the fog, is that achieved only by the mature playwright.

Perhaps *Long Day's Journey* is most remarkable for what it is not. It is not a drama of action: "It austerely ignores almost every means, including action, by which the usual play interests an audience."[6] And it is not a drama of violence: although the emotions involved find violent expression in words, they remain within the bounds of "normal" family life. It is not, therefore, a drama of extremes: the "Lower Depths" of *The Iceman* and the domestic depravity of *Mourning Becomes Electra* have been left behind; and the mystical ecstasy of *Lazarus* appears only as a remembrance of things past. *Long Day's Journey* describes the mid-world of middle-class family life, and its greatness lies in its simple domestication both of tragic emotion and of human insight. The impact of the mother's dope addiction is intensified by the very fact that there is no "abnormal" reason for it. And, when in the last act, the father thoughtlessly denounces Dante Gabriel Rossetti as a "dope-fiend," the irony becomes obvious.

The positive excellence of the play consists not in the plot but in the characterization. The four chief characters are probably the four most memorable in all O'Neill's works—with the addition of Ephraim Cabot in *Desire Under the Elms*. The father embodies the qualities of petty dictator characteristic of all O'Neill's fathers, but he remains more human and more understandable. Mary Tyrone embodies the qualities of unworldly innocence typical both of American womanhood of the nineteenth century and of all Christian mariolatry as well—as her name suggests. Jamie Tyrone re-incarnates the Mephistopheles of Dion Anthony, but without the artificiality of a mask. And Edmund Tyrone, seemingly passive, develops steadily, although unobtrusively, during the play until at the end he achieves what O'Neill had prophesied for his autobiographical hero: "the birth of a soul."

Although *Long Day's Journey* abjures physical action, it dramatizes psychological action to a superlative degree. Mary Tyrone gradually regresses from the sunlight world of reality to the fog-bound world of dope and dreams. As the play begins, she *"smiles affectionately"*; but, as it ends *"she stares before her in a sad dream."* But her son Edmund, in almost perfect counterpoint, begins as "mama's baby, papa's pet," and ends as the only member of the family wholly clear headed and emotionally unwarped. For him—as for the author and the audience—the play has been "a play of discovery, like Oedipus." And for Edmund Tyrone the commitment to the sanitarium will provide a release from the family furies and ultimately a "journey into light."

Meanwhile Edmund Tyrone's psychological journey into light is motivated by his conflicts with—and his final understanding of—both his father and his brother. At first he and Jamie make common cause against the tyranny of the father, and the first part of the play dramatizes their guerilla warfare against his miserliness and his pompous self-importance. "Old Gaspard, the miser" and "the Beautiful Voice" stand between them and (as they believe) happiness and self-fulfillment. But in the final act James Tyrone explains to Edmund the ancestral causes of his miserliness and his theatrical manner, and Edmund *"Moved, stares at his father with understanding—slowly.* 'I'm glad you've told me this, Papa. I know you a lot better now.' " The sources of his conflict with his father have been clarified, and Edmund begins to see the light.

But the conflict of father and son—which seems to be the source of Edmund's confusion, and which the father's confession illuminates so clearly—is not the true source of the tragedy, nor does it mark the climax of the play. The conflict of Edmund with his brother Jamie is much more fundamental, more subtle, and more significant. And the discovery of the sources of this conflict —indeed, the very discovery that this conflict exists at all—marks the true climax of the play. It provides the final moment of illumination, and of tragic catharsis. In the last act, after the confessions of the father and of Edmund, Jamie comes home drunk. And after a comic account of his maudlin evening with "Fat Violet," he suddenly tells Edmund what "I don't want to hear——." In a burst of drunken self-revelation he explains to his brother the subconscious cause of Edmund's "consumption." Jamie—the jealous older brother, the cynical tempter of innocent youth, Pan, Mephistopheles, Cain—explains why, subconsciously, he has sought to kill the life-giving illusions of his younger brother.

This conflict of older brother with younger—of Cain with Abel, of cynical materialist with aspiring artist—goes far beyond any simple conflict of character. It illuminates the conflict of two philosophies of life—two philosophies which *seem* the same; which James Tyrone, Sr., believes to be the same; and which many critics of O'Neill have believed to be identical. The conflict between the cynical negations preached by Jamie and the tragic transcendence of these negations, which lies at the heart of all Edmund Tyrone's (Eugene O'Neill's) dramas, is, indeed, the subject finally illuminated by *Long Day's Journey.*

Sophus Winther has pointed out that the poetic philosophy of the autobiographical Edmund Tyrone constitutes one of the main themes of the drama.[7] By far the most "literary" of O'Neill's plays, it contains many passages of quotation from O'Neill's favorite authors and it even includes several lists of these authors, both in its stage directions and in the dialogue itself. And the greatest—indeed, the only—criticism of Edmund voiced by his father, concerns the "rotten" books which he reads: "That damned library of yours: Voltaire, Rousseau, Schopenhauer, Nietzsche, Ibsen! Atheists, fools, and madmen! And your poets! This Dowson, and this Baudelaire, and Swinburne, and Oscar Wilde, and Whitman and Poe! Whoremongers and degenerates! Pah!"

The father emphasizes that he considers Edmund's philosophy to be as "degenerate" as Jamie's: "There's little choice between the philosophy you learned from Broadway loafers, and the one Edmund got from his books."

But just before this wholesale condemnation, by the father, of the evil "philosophy" of both sons, Edmund had attacked Jamie. "*Parodying his brother's cynicism*," he had exclaimed: "Christ, if I felt the way you do——!" And Jamie had replied: "I thought you did. Your poetry isn't very cheery." Thus Edmund had emphasized his rejection of his brother's cynicism as early as the second act, and his brother had pretended surprise. But in the last act, Jamie, drunk, explains the subconscious causes of his difference from Edmund, and he confesses that he had led Edmund into temptation on purpose, to make him fall: "Made getting drunk romantic. Made whores fascinating vampires, instead of poor, stupid, diseased slobs they really are." By emphasizing the radical difference between his own mephistophelian cynicism and Edmund's genuine tragic idealism, Jamie clarifies the values and the meaning of the play.

This emphatic statement of the difference between the evil of Jamie and the good of Edmund is doubly important because it clarifies the apparent confusion between good and evil suggested by Larry Slade's rejection of "truth" in *The Iceman*. There is as radical a difference between the "drunkenness" of Jamie and that of Edmund as there is between the romantic philosophies of despair and of transcendence. And, when Edmund recounts to his father "some high spots" of his memories, he emphasizes his own mystical experiences: "I became drunk with the beauty and singing rhythm of it, and for a moment I lost myself——actually lost my life. I was set free!" In this moment of transcendence he experienced "the birth of a soul," which would result in his ultimate triumph. And he then felt closer to his father—who had experienced similar moments of triumph but had forgotten them —than he did to his brother, who had always remained lost in the night.

The psychological "long day's journey into night," which gives title and direction to the play, is a different journey for each of its characters. For the mother, it is a sad journey into the fog of dope and dream. For Jamie, it is a hopeless journey into the night of cynicism and despair. For the father, it is a tragic journey down the wrong road, away from an earlier triumph. But for Edmund, it is, prophetically, a journey beyond night. And dramatically, the story of these conflicting characters and of their contrasting journeys is the essence of the play.)

But, philosophically, the play focuses on the Transcendental idealism of Edmund Tyrone. And his tragedy is not that of defeat, but of a suffering which leads to illumination. Like the others, he also journeys through the fog and the night. But, unlike them, he has seen—and will again see—beyond the illusions which surround him. And ideally the play reaches its climax in his eloquent account of his own experiences of transcendence, ending with a metaphor of illumination not unlike that of Emerson's famous essay on "Illusions": ". . . Then the moment of ecstatic freedom came. The peace, the end of the quest, the last harbor, the joy of belonging. . . . Like a saint's vision of beatitude. Like the veil of things as they seem drawn back by an unseen hand. For a second you see—and seeing the secret, are the secret. For a second there is meaning! Then the hand lets the veil fall and you are alone, lost in the fog again. . . ." Even if only "for a second," there has been the experience of meaning.

III A Moon for the Misbegotten

A Moon for the Misbegotten is perhaps the most unusual drama written by a playwright whose dramas were all unusual. It has been highly praised and wholly damned, and no agreement is in sight. Joseph Wood Krutch (who praised most of O'Neill's work) condemned it; Doris Falk called it "the veriest scratching in rat's alley"; Carlotta Monterey O'Neill "loathed" it. Yet O'Neill himself considered it "top flight," and the Gelbs have agreed with him; Mary McCarthy (who disliked most of O'Neill's work) paid "homage to its mythic powers" and to "the element of transcendence jutting up in it."[8] Clearly, this last work of America's first dramatist is no ordinary play.

When *A Moon,* first produced by the Theatre Guild in 1947, failed completely, it was withdrawn before it could reach Broadway. In 1953, when it was produced in Stockholm, it won critical acclaim. And in 1957 it finally reached Broadway, but survived only briefly. And the physical reason for its theatrical failure has always been obvious: the heroine is described as *"so oversize for a woman that she is almost a freak."* No actress with the physical qualifications for Josie Hogan could ever hope for any other role, except perhaps in a circus side-show. Josie is clearly a grotesque, resembling physically the "Fat Violet" described (with grotesque humor) by James Tyrone in *Long Day's Journey.*

But the physical nature of the heroine is also reflected in the artistic and psychological nature of the play. Josie Hogan is further described as *"more powerful than any but an exceptionally strong man. But there is no mannish quality about her. She is all woman."* Besides being "almost a freak," she is a woman whose nature is self-contradictory—a kind of goddess who is nevertheless frustrated by her own "oversize" mortality. Born "different," she longs only to be ordinary. When James Tyrone urges her to "be yourself," she wishes only to be loved in the ordinary manner of womankind. The play, therefore, dramatizes the self-contradictory nature of mankind.

To dramatize this self-contradiction, the three chief characters are all described as grotesques: the oversize heroine; her undersize father whose *"little blue eyes with bleached lashes and eyebrows remind one of a white pig's";* and James Tyrone, Jr., the drunken prodigal who has passed beyond the hope of redemption. But Josie and her father are mythical grotesques, invented to act out an American Gothic drama; while James Tyrone, Jr., is Jamie O'Neill, all too human and wholly actual. The uniqueness of the play lies partly in this juxtaposition of grotesque myth with autobiographical actuality. It is almost incredible, but it is also real.

Besides mixing the grotesquely mythical with the autobiographically factual, *A Moon* combines the farcical with the tragic, the illusory with the real. As the plot unfolds, the audience—and also the characters—remain confused as to what the real truth is. In fact the play becomes an exercise in the uncovering of this elusive "truth." Each of the three characters tries to trick the others, and none is ever quite sure what the true intentions of the others are. For that matter, none is ever quite sure what his own intentions are. Each pretends to be something different from what he really is, and only at the end is "the truth" partially revealed. Critics have condemned the "crudity" of this technique that fails to reveal fully the truth.

But this apparent crudity is wholly intentional; it is the essence of the technique by which O'Neill sought to dramatize the discovery of meaning. In the last act of this play, "the veil of things" (to borrow the words of Edmund Tyrone in *Long Day's Journey*) seems briefly to be "drawn aside, and for a second, there is meaning."

The essence of the plot is marked by its apparent confusion. Hogan and his daughter are tenants on a farm owned by Tyrone. All three are Irish, and they heartily enjoy one another's company. But, being Irish, they enjoy making fun of one another, and they make it a point of pride to trick one another. Tyrone has promised not to sell their farm. But he is now offered three times its worth by a Standard Oil tycoon who does not relish the Hogans as neighbors. Moreover, Tyrone's father will not advance him any money, and so he now threatens to sell the farm, after all. He likes the Hogans, but he is also human. What are his true intentions?

Meanwhile, Josie Hogan loves Tyrone, and he even loves her "after his fashion." He loves her true "self"—that is, her Irishness, and her genuine womanliness. But he is also a profligate, who knows that he could never make a good husband. And besides, he idealizes her, in contrast to the "tarts" whom he has always known. But she is willing to do anything to get him, and so she plots to get him drunk and to seduce him. And her fathers sees a chance to trap Tyrone into marriage, so that, as one of the family, his farm will legally become theirs. Josie, of course, will have no part of this trickery. But, when her father makes her believe that Tyrone really intends to sell the farm, she agrees in anger to seduce Tyrone before witnesses, so that he will have to marry her. Nevertheless, when he finally comes to her in his drunken despair and wishes only to confess his sins and guilt to her, she takes pity on him. Overcome by his sincerity and by his tragic need, she forgets both her father's devious schemes and her own desire for his physical love. After his confession he goes to sleep on her breast, finally at peace.

This plot is simple to summarize. But as it unfolds on the stage, it seems like a maze full of false clues and blind alleys. In the beginning each character is introduced—and each introduces himself—as the opposite of what he actually is. Hogan's eyes outwardly resemble a pig's, yet they twinkle with humor within.

Josie, who talks like a wanton through the early acts, only gradually admits that this is only a pretense invented to cover up the humiliation of her oversize body. But Tyrone is obviously happy at the opportunity to be himself with these two pretenders, as he, in his turn, pretends to be their villainous landlord.

The strangeness of the play lies in the techniques by which the inner contradictions of the characters are suggested. To the technique of purposeful confusion, O'Neill added the technique of melodramatic exaggeration. At the beginning of the third act James Tyrone *"sings sneeringly half under his breath a snatch from an old sob song, popular in the 1890's:* "And baby's cries can't waken her in the baggage coach ahead." Then gradually, by fits and starts, he confesses to Josie the source of his innermost guilt. His mother had died in California, and he had brought her body to the East for burial. But on the train he got drunk and had spent the trip in a drawing room with a prostitute, while his dead mother lay "in the baggage coach ahead." On arrival in New York he had been too drunk even to attend her funeral. Thus, by a series of grotesque actions, he had betrayed his mother and had disgraced himself. And the violent incongruity of these actions is emphasized by the crude absurdity of the "old sob song."

"In moments of violent stress," O'Neill believed, "life copies melodrama." Now this play self-consciously copied melodrama in order to suggest the violence of these emotions. The technique is intentionally crude, and the story is melodramatically incredible. But, of course, it tells the literal truth about James O'Neill, Jr. O'Neill's life was almost too melodramatic to be believed, and this play has also seemed melodramatic.

In the final analysis, however, it is not the autobiographical character of James Tyrone, Jr., that dominates *A Moon*, but the mythical character of Josie Hogan. And the play's success (or failure) finally depends on the degree to which she is realized in the reader's imagination. Obviously a creature of myth, she combines all the contradictory elements of the eternal feminine, which each of O'Neill's earlier heroines had embodied separately. A primitive creature of the earth, strong and inarticulate, she suggests Cybel, the earth-mother of *The Great God Brown*. But, forced by her own freakish physique to remain unloved, she can only day-dream and pretend comically to be the eternal prostitute.

And when James Tyrone's genuine affection for her seems about to fulfill her desire, his compelling need to idealize her purity finally forces her to accept her own limitations and to forego her dreams. A woman with a monstrous physique, she remains the reluctant virgin, accepting the strange role of a mother-confessor to a sinner damned beyond hope of redemption. And all these contradictions of her character seem almost too great to be borne. Whether they are also too great to be believed is, of course, the crucial question.

In the final act of this last play, all the contradictions of O'Neill's contradictory life and dramatic art combine to produce a single unforgettable image. Once again, life and art copy melodrama: *"It is dawn. . . . Josie sits in the same position on the steps, her arms around Tyrone. He is still asleep, his head on her breast."* Consciously intended (like the earlier "old sob song") to suggest the melodramatically absurd, this tableau recalls that universal cliché: "Came the Dawn!" But the sentimentality of the cliché only emphasizes the irony of the situation, and the tragedy that has preceded it. In their long journey through the night, these two have passed beyond hope: "It was my mistake," Josie says. "I thought there was still hope." But they have also experienced the intensity of beauty: "I was glad of the excuse to stay awake and enjoy the beauty of the moon," Josie says. And Tyrone, as he gradually awakens from his drunken sleep to this new dawn, comments: "God seems to be putting on quite a display." Then he exclaims cynically: "I like Belasco better. Rise of curtain, Act-Four Stuff!" But he ends with the emphatic affirmation: "God, it's beautiful, Josie!—I'll never forget it."

CHAPTER 8

Greatness and Limitations

WHEN ALL HAS BEEN SAID, O'Neill remains an enigma. His plays have been acted and read, the story of his life told, but the essential question remains unanswered. Like the haunted heroes whom he created, his ghost, bowing remotely, seems to haunt the theater of the mind. Unlike Hemingway and Faulkner, who have been soundly applauded and clearly defined, he remains unknown. He was a major dramatist, certainly, and his historical importance remains unquestioned. But how good was he?—or how great? Critics do not agree.

This disagreement has existed from the beginning. In the early 1920's many hailed him as the greatest modern dramatist; others dismissed him contemptuously. In 1946 his friend George Jean Nathan could assert that "the great body of his work has a size and significance not remotely approached by any other American." But two years later the London *Times Literary Supplement* declared that "O'Neill's world is a bestiary full of vulpine animals and crushed worms," and scornfully described "the mass of undisciplined emotions and jejune opinions which appear in his plays."[1] If these opposing judgments seem like mere drumbeating and name-calling, at least they prove that he has aroused strong emotions. Whatever else he was, he was never dull. But because there has always been disagreement, it may be helpful to itemize the praise and the blame.

I   *Greatness*

First of all, O'Neill was "the founder of the American drama." Before him no playwright of such importance had emerged. By his influence and example, he practically created native drama in America. In granting him this distinction, critics are almost unanimous. His historical importance is clear.

This phenomenon is remarkable enough. But after O'Neill had achieved fame in the 1920's, many other American dramatists won distinction. Some were his contemporaries, like Maxwell Anderson and Elmer Rice; others, like Tennessee Williams and Arthur Miller, followed the path he explored. But no contemporary or follower has approached his stature, and now, a decade after his death, his leadership is unquestioned. Nobody agrees in the selection of the "greatest American novelist" or the "greatest American poet," but O'Neill remains "our greatest dramatist." This continuing pre-eminence is even more remarkable.

But the American drama has had a short history. And beyond the drama, O'Neill must be judged by the standards of literature. Besides being a dramatist, he was necessarily a writer—but how good a writer was he? The disagreement begins here. Many literary critics consider him important only as a dramatist. An earlier critic of the London *Times* asserted that "his greatest handicap is that he is so little a writer." And John Mason Brown agreed: "Though he possesses the tragic vision, he cannot claim the tragic tongue." Nevertheless, his plays have always been widely read. They have been reprinted by the millions, and have appeared in all the anthologies. And critically, the second book written about him—and the most enthusiastic—was by a man who had never seen his plays on the stage. Even now many people would rather read than see his dramas. In spite of disagreement, he has also achieved acclaim as a man of letters.

If O'Neill was primarily a dramatist, and if he often seemed to lack a literary style, it was partly because he concerned himself so immediately with the raw materials of life. The autobiographical nature of his writing has become increasingly apparent since his death: he wrote directly out of his own life and emotions. Of course this material is reflected most clearly in his late autobiographical plays, but his life also shaped his early plays. And the modern biographical approach to his work has yielded significant insights.

When read consecutively and when considered in relation to his life, all his dramas seem to fall into a significant pattern. Beyond their individual qualities, they seem to describe the successive stages of a spiritual quest. Recent critics have recognized this, and have sought to describe it in different ways. Like Melville's actual and fictional voyages, O'Neill's plays, both autobiographical and symbolic, seem to suggest his continuing search for salvation, or for "meaning." They are autobiographical, that is, both in a literal and in a spiritual sense.

But many modern readers distrust all spiritual quests. The "new critics," especially, have refused to value any work of art for qualities outside itself. And this "new criticism," with its strict emphasis on formal unity and literary style, has been particularly hard on O'Neill. Nevertheless, if the only test is that of individual excellence, his final dramas have passed that test successfully. After having achieved historic recognition and after having followed his own autobiographical quest to the end, he wrote the two plays which most critics have recognized as his best. Not content with past achievements, and combining his life-long quest for meaning with his search for artistic excellence, he wrote his best plays last.

This phenomenon is, perhaps, the most remarkable of all. No other American and few writers in history have written their greatest works at the end of their careers. In America, indeed, a common criticism of our artists has been that they have often failed to develop beyond a certain point; all too often, they have regressed. Among O'Neill's American contemporaries who also won the Nobel Prize, Sinclair Lewis clearly deteriorated after writing *Arrowsmith*, and John Steinbeck after writing *The Grapes of Wrath*. Even Melville, whose earlier quest resembles O'Neill's, wrote *Moby Dick* in mid-career, and after that only minor masterpieces. Alone among his contemporaries and compatriots, O'Neill continued to grow spiritually and to improve artistically to the very end.

Until his final dramas were published, he had seemed to belong to an earlier generation. In the 1920's he had given historic expression to "the modern temper," with its loss of faith and spiritual confusion. But his comparative failure in the 1930's followed by long silence, gave the impression that he too had deteriorated—sunk in some modern slough of despond. Only after his death did a second generation realize that, by virtue of his final dramas, he belonged to it also. Not only had he continued to grow, but his individual growth coincided with that of the modern world. From the sentimental self-pity of "the lost generation,", to the more astringent pessimism of modern existential philosophy, the world changed; and O'Neill changed with it.

But even before his final period, O'Neill had been widely acclaimed by the leading dramatists and critics of foreign countries. From the first Irishman who in 1923 rated him above Shaw and Synge, to the series of books about him in foreign languages published in the last two decades, he has been recognized even more as a major figure in world literature than as the leading American dramatist. Indeed, his world reputation has probably exceeded his American one from the time that his first plays became known. Much more than Lewis or Hemingway, who were chosen for the Nobel Prize primarily because of their American reputations, O'Neill has spoken directly to a world audience. This is his last, and perhaps his most important, claim to greatness.

II *Limitations*

But there have always been limitations. Or more precisely, there have always been emphatic denials to his claims to greatness. The only specific criticism, indeed, has concerned his style or skill as a writer. Other criticisms have been total; they have condemned the very substance and quality of his accomplishment. And many of these have paraphrased the condemnation (just quoted): of "the mass of undisciplined emotions and jejune opinions which appear in his plays." They have called O'Neill a "melodramatist," and coined the phrase "melodramadness." They have attacked his "sensationalism" and his "hysterical" emotions. And they have dismissed his ideas as "negligible," repeating the classic criticism made about another romantic writer: "he is a child when he thinks." In short, most negative criticism has not tried to define his "limitations"; rather, it has denied his excellence altogether.

The most articulate critic of O'Neill, who has published five articles about him, has been Eric Bentley. And the most typical of his articles is entitled: "Trying to Like O'Neill."[2] Try as he will, the negative critic has simply been unable to persuade himself to "like" O'Neill at all. Ultimately, of course, this "liking" is a matter of taste or temperament. But by examining the tastes and temperaments of those who have disliked O'Neill, one can learn a good deal about his limitations—and perhaps also about his greatness.

When Mr. Bentley was engaged to direct *The Iceman Cometh*, he began by cutting: "To get at the core of reality in *The Iceman*, you have to cut away the rotten fruit of unreality around it." So he cut what he considered "rotten" in O'Neill—all that was mystical and mythical. By "a systematic underlining of all that is realistic . . . the comedy was sharpened, the sentiment purified." But in spite of this "purification," Bentley's audience disliked the play, and he was thereby confirmed in his own dislike. Having cut what was most typically O'Neillian from O'Neill's major play, he still found himself unable to approve the dramatist.

The essential antipathy of negative critics to O'Neill, *qua* O'Neill, has caused much confusion. Mr. Bentley, for instance, confidently asserted that "the more he attempts, the less he succeeds." Every critic is entitled to his opinion, but this subjective opinion is particularly confusing because it seems the exact opposite of demonstrable fact. For, in actual practice, O'Neill's greatest successes have been his longest plays, in which he has attempted most: in terms of theatrical success, *The Iceman* and *Strange Interlude* have enjoyed the longest runs on the New York stage; and in terms of critical success, *Long Day's Journey, The Iceman,* and (among the earlier plays) *Mourning Becomes Electra* have been most highly praised. What Mr. Bentley really means is that the more he sees of O'Neill, the less he likes him. But for most readers and critics, the more O'Neill has attempted, the better he has succeeded.

It is, precisely, the essential O'Neill that has aroused the greatest antagonism, as well as the greatest enthusiasm, among both critics and readers: not the "realism" of his characters and settings, nor the "purity" of his sentiments and emotions, nor, certainly, the clarity of his ideas. Rather the psychological strangeness of his characters, and the sensational depth of their emotions, and the very mystical symbolism of their "ideas"—these have appealed to most audiences at the same time that they have aroused "dislike" in others. O'Neill's greatness, that is, is almost identical with his limitations.

This critical truth was first suggested by one of O'Neill's most emphatic detractors. Describing him as "the melodramatist: the seeker after sensational effect," Francis Fergusson nevertheless recognized that "his naïve belief in emotion is related to a price-less quality, which one may call the histrionic sincerity, the essence of mummery."[3] Although O'Neill "abandoned himself to emotion" and although "he never found any discipline" to give artistic form, he did succeed in fascinating his audiences where other more artistic and disciplined dramatists had failed. Perhaps, indeed, because O'Neill rejected all the artistic conventions and traditional techniques by which a "good" dramatist should interest his audience, he succeeded in enthralling the masses. Although Mr. Fergusson emphatically believed that he was a bad dramatist, he saw that "the man O'Neill was very close to a vast audience."

One of the reasons for these subjective dislikes and condemna-tions of O'Neill has been suggested by an Italian critic. Camillo Pellizzi has pointed to the "Catholic, anti-Puritan, Irish" element in O'Neill's work, which made him "the enemy of Anglo-Saxon race and religion."[4] And his temperamental anti-Puritanism has contributed to his rejection by typically British critics and audiences: the traditional reticence of the Anglo-Saxon tem-perament, which has always rejected the "undisciplined" expres-sion of strong emotion, has caused much of the negative criticism. And this "Anglo-Saxon" reticence has also influenced anglophile and academic critics in America, whose "moral sense and fineness of taste rebel" against O'Neill's uninhibited emotionalism.

Mr. Pellizzi went on to define the positive aspect of O'Neill's "anti-Puritan . . . psychological quality" as *passionateness.* This "passionate" quality has seemed mere undisciplined emotion to the Anglo-Saxon temperament, but it has appealed to Latin audiences throughout the world. If it has been one cause of O'Neill's "limitation," it has also contributed to his greatness. But the Italian critic did not go far enough: this "passionateness" is only one half of "the essential O'Neill." The other half is defined by the artistic and psychological use which O'Neill made of his passionate emotions. And this use is suggested by the word "mysticism." If O'Neill's dramatic characters gave passionate expression to their emotions, they also learned to use (or to sublimate) these emotions in order to achieve a mystical understanding, or illumination. And this quality of mysticism has often aroused as much "dislike" among O'Neill's critics as his "passionateness."

The most famous attack on O'Neill was made by Bernard DeVoto at the time of the Nobel award.[5] It condemned, not his emotionalism, but the vague grandiosity of his ideas. After writing some good early plays (DeVoto admitted), "Mr. O'Neill then dived into the infinite." Yet, DeVoto continued, "What seem to be immensities turn out to be one-syllable ideas and mostly wrong at that." And although DeVoto nowhere mentioned "mysticism," he prefaced his attack on O'Neill with an even more violent attack on Rabindranath Tagore, whose immensities also seemed to him both grandiose and "mostly wrong at that." For DeVoto was a practical-minded American critic.

What have seemed the faults and limitations of O'Neill's writing to a minority of critics, then, have also seemed O'Neill's greatest virtues to a majority. Just as his passionate emotions have appealed to Latin and Continental readers, who have always distrusted the inhibitions of the Anglo-Saxon temperament, so his mysticism has appealed to religious-minded and Oriental readers, who have distrusted American practicality. Much of O'Neill's greatness lies in his appeal beyond the limits of his own country and language to the peoples of other nations and continents. Recently a Hindu scholar has suggested that O'Neill's personal and artistic development "combined in itself the various elements of both Western and Eastern mysticism."[6] Renouncing the conventions of traditional American and Anglo-Saxon audiences, O'Neill limited his appeal to them, but appealed beyond them to the audiences of the world.

III *Theory of Tragedy: Emotion and Transcendence*

The reasons both for O'Neill's greatness and for his limitations lie implicit in his theory of tragedy. Although he never proclaimed this formally, or developed it in detail, he suggested the outlines of it in early letters and interviews. Moreover, this theory guided his dramatic practice throughout his career, and it was realized progressively in the composition of his plays. But he was so little the philosopher that its fundamental importance has often been overlooked. The earlier chapters of this book have suggested the literary origins of his theory and the pattern which he realized in his plays. But there were certain underlying principles.

O'Neill's theory of tragedy consisted of two positive principles and of a negative one. First, he asserted that our emotions are of primary importance, both in theory and in practice. Second, that the expression of our emotions, through the medium of tragic drama, is a "life-giving" process, leading to a "deeper spiritual understanding." But third, because our emotions are primary, and the expression and understanding of them is of first importance, it follows that our thoughts and even our actions are of secondary importance.

In an interview published in 1922, he asserted: "Our emotions are a better guide than our thoughts. Our emotions are instinctive. They are the result not only of our individual experiences, but of the experiences of the whole human race through the ages. They are the deep undercurrent, whereas our thoughts are often only the small individual surface reactions. Truth usually goes deep. So it reaches you through your emotions."[7] He repeated this belief in the primary importance of the emotions in later years, and he never greatly qualified it. Since it is both clear and emphatic and since it guided his whole practice of tragedy, it is worth considering in detail.

His theory was not a scientific principle based upon demonstrable fact (although it asserted a familiar psychological hypothesis). It was, rather, an affirmation of belief, and of value: "our emotions are a *better guide*." It was a statement of faith, and, as such, it cannot be proved scientifically, or argued logically. It can only be contradicted by a counter-statement of an opposite belief, such as: "our emotions are not to be trusted." When Francis Fergusson accused O'Neill of "a naïve belief in emotion," he was making such an opposite statement; for all belief is, by definition, "naïve." It is not scientific, and it is not intellectual.

O'Neill's fundamental belief in emotion, however, placed him in sharp conflict with the dominant beliefs of the modern, Western world. For modern scientific philosophy has always asserted the primary importance of our thoughts (*cogito ergo sum*) and of our actions (pragmatism). But O'Neill contradicted this philosophy; he reaffirmed the age-old belief, typical of the Eastern world, in the primacy of emotion. For, in the eyes of the Orient, our Western emphasis on logical thought and practical action has always seemed "naïve." And from his earliest years O'Neill had been attracted to this Oriental belief.

Moreover, he clearly recognized the religious nature of this belief. Recalling the religious origins of tragedy in Greece, he wished to recapture the emotional values of the art for the modern world. Writing to George Jean Nathan in 1923, he protested: "Reason has no business in the theater anyway, any more than it has in church. They are both either below—or above it."[8] He valued the tragic theater as a kind of church, and he prophesied "a theater returned to its highest and sole significant function as a temple where the religion of poetical interpretation and symbolic celebration of life is communicated to human beings."[9] That is, he believed that tragedy should induce a kind of religious experience.

His theory of tragic emotion brought him into conflict with two groups. First, he joyously attacked the American philistines who believed that "tragedy" is merely "morbid" and "depressing." At first this group included his own father; and he answered it with the defiant exclamation: "Life is a tragedy, hurrah!" But then he explained: if tragedy brings physical defeat (as the philistines argue), it also brings spiritual exaltation, through the recognition that man's tragic struggle is like that of Prometheus—although destined to defeat by the nature of things, it gives greatness to man's effort to learn the secrets of life. "A man wills his own defeat when he pursues the unattainable. But the struggle is his success. . . . Such a figure is necessarily tragic, but to me he is exhilarating."[10]

So far, so good: O'Neill was reaffirming the traditional values of tragedy. And historically, this was his great accomplishment: he reclaimed the spiritual values of tragedy for a nation concerned chiefly with material things and for a generation concerned chiefly with entertainment. But, in his rebellion against American materialism and in his scorn for the superficialities of the literature and theater of his time, he went on to attack all "materialism" in such a way as to minimize the pragmatic values of man's struggle. And, by his exclusive concern with emotion, he progressively excluded the element of action, upon which tragedy has traditionally depended for its most dramatic effects. His scorn for "the American dream of material things" led him, by contrast, to dramatize those unrealistic "pipe dreams" which are wholly divorced from reason and from action.

The peculiar nature of O'Neill's theory and practice of tragedy is defined by the extreme nature of his belief in the value of emotion and by his corresponding disbelief in the value of practical action. His early plays had concerned themselves more with the external realities of setting and action, and it is significant that critics who dislike O'Neill have usually preferred the early *Emperor Jones* and *Anna Christie*. But beginning with *The Hairy Ape*, O'Neill's tragic heroes progressively insisted that action is relatively unimportant because: "Dis ting's in your inside." And O'Neill's tragedies progressively dramatized conflicts of inner emotion rather than of external action.

The typical hero of an O'Neill tragedy struggles and suffers inevitable defeat, like all tragic heroes. But, unlike the traditional tragic hero, he does not struggle actively against an external enemy, nor does he seek victory over a physical antagonist. Rather he struggles psychologically and seeks victory over the enemy within. He does not go forth to fight against some tyrannical "Creon"; he struggles against the tyranny of his own contradictory emotions. And his greatest victory (as in *Long Day's Journey*) consists of his final achievement of perfect understanding and fellow-feeling for a tyrannical father or for a hostile older brother. By means of tragedy, he transcends his own selfish emotions and achieves illumination.

"It seems to me," O'Neill wrote in 1922, "that man is much the same creature, with the same primal emotions and ambitions and motives, the same powers and the same weaknesses, as in the time when the Aryan race started toward Europe from the slopes of the Himalayas. He has become better acquainted with those powers and those weaknesses, and he is learning ever so slowly how to control them."[11] His tragic dramas consciously described man's struggle to become acquainted with his inner emotions and, ideally, to control them. This inner exploration and this spiritual control were the primary purposes of his tragic writing. This was also the age-old purpose of mysticism, which had begun "on the slopes of the Himalayas."

The mysticism of O'Neill's theory of tragedy—which idealized the exploration of man's inner emotions and the transformation of them, rather than the more common Western ideal of exploring man's conscious mind and controlling his external actions—has caused most of the negative criticism of his plays. Rationalists (like Mary McCarthy) criticize mystical emotion because it is not rational; pragmatists (like Bernard DeVoto) criticize it because it is not practical; and both have attacked O'Neill with all the enthusiasm of religious believers railing against an opposing creed.

But O'Neill's exclusive belief in emotion and the extreme nature of his mysticism have also, to average audiences, limited the appeal of his tragedies. They have resulted in a kind of introversion and in a corresponding lack of concern for external things. This anti-pragmatism contributed to the failure of his great Cycle of plays dealing with American history. And finally, this introversion led away from action to a kind of "Fatal Balance" (as Doris Falk has described it), in which the protagonists of his final plays seem to suffer from a kind of stasis, or paralysis of the will. They achieve illumination, but it leads not to action—only to a new emotion exalted by the experience of tragedy.

O'Neill's exclusive concern with emotion resulted also in an exclusive interest in tragedy. It has been said that "life is a tragedy to him who feels, but a comedy to him who thinks." And O'Neill, the modern writer of pure tragedy, contrasts sharply with George Bernard Shaw, the modern master of comedy. Although these two dominate the drama of modern times, they resemble each other in few other ways. O'Neill's tragedies dramatized the inner feelings of men; Shaw's comedies dramatized their thoughts and actions. The intellectual brilliance which distinguished Shaw was lacking in O'Neill, and the depth of feeling which distinguished O'Neill was lacking in Shaw. In the specialization of modern man, each developed the primary virtue lacking in the other.

But the unique quality of O'Neill does not lie in his modernity. Although his tragedy was typically American and although it sought to dramatize the "sickness of today," it also remembered the mysticism of the ancient East. Living in the most modern age of the most practical nation at the farthest West of the world, O'Neill followed a dimly remembered but not unfamiliar path. Marked by the psycho-logic of the emotions, it led through a series of tragedies designed for "the theater of tomorrow" and to a goal not unlike that of the most ancient religions of the East. O'Neill described all men's hopes as "pipe dreams"—as the illusions of Maya, and the source of all life. And he described man's goal as a mystical experience resembling that of Nirvana —"the discovery of meaning" through the transcendence of all hopes and selfish illusions.

O'Neill's final greatness lies in his appeal beyond the modernity of his America to the timeless element in all civilization. His *Long Day's Journey* realized a tragedy typically American, but universal also. His dramas have proved equally popular on Broadway, and in Stockholm, Tokyo, and Buenos Aires. One of the major figures of American literature, he is also one of the major dramatists of the modern world.

Notes and References

Preface

1. Heinrich Straumann, *American Literature in the Twentieth Century* (London, 1951), p. 163.

Chapter One

1. Doris Alexander, *The Tempering of Eugene O'Neill* (New York, 1962), p. 12;—hereinafter "Alexander."

2. Arthur and Barbara Gelb, *O'Neill* (New York, 1962)—hereinafter "Gelb"—describe the operation as occurring many years after Eugene's birth. Miss Alexander describes it as occurring eighteen months before his birth.

3. Gelb, pp. 220-25.

4. John Henry Raleigh, "O'Neill's *Long Day's Journey* and New England Irish-Catholicism," *Partisan Review*, XXVI (Fall, 1959), 573-92.

5. When William Butler Yeats visited Harvard University in the early 1930's, the present writer was assigned to interview him. He seemed taciturn until O'Neill's name was mentioned, but then discoursed enthusiastically on O'Neill's plays.

6. Alexander, p. 24.

7. See Earl H. Rovit, "American Literature and 'The American Experience,'" *American Quarterly*, III (Summer, 1961), 115-25.

8. Gelb, p. 155.

9. *Ibid.*, p. 88.

10. Doris M. Alexander, "Eugene O'Neill and *Light on the Path*," *Modern Drama*, III (December, 1960), 260-67.

11. Alexander, p. 232.

12. Allen Churchill, "Portrait of a Nobel Prize Winner as a Bum," *Esquire*, XLVII (June, 1957), 98-101.

13. Croswell Bowen, "The Black Irishman," *PM*, November 3, 1946.

14. Gelb, p. 131.

15. *Ibid.*, p. 616.

16. *Ibid.*, p. 623.

17. See A. A. Nethercot, "The Psychoanalyzing of Eugene O'Neill," *Modern Drama*, III (December, 1960), 242-56; and (February, 1961), 357-72.

18. Quoted in Mary Mullett, "The Extraordinary Story of Eugene O'Neill," *American Magazine*, XCIV (November, 1922), 34 and 112-20. (This valuable "interview" is not reprinted in Cargill.)

19. Letter, reprinted in Cargill, *O'Neill and His Plays*, p. 101.

20. See Cargill, p. 257.

21. See Edwin A. Engel, *The Haunted Heroes of Eugene O'Neill,* pp. 63-95.
22. This "gold" play was to be entitled "The Career of Bessie Bowen." (Letter to F. I. Carpenter, March 24, 1945.)
23. Gelb, p. 599.
24. *Ibid.,* p. 598.
25. See Cargill, p. 282.
26. Gelb, p. 4.

Chapter Two

1. A. H. Quinn, *Representative American Plays* (4th ed., New York, 1928), p. 966.
2. S. K. Winther, *Eugene O'Neill* (New York, 1934), p. 8.
3. See Barrett Clark, *Eugene O'Neill* (New York, 1929), p. 181. "The most successful thing I ever did. I think I've got it just right. It *is,* from my view point."
4. H. Frenz, "Eugene O'Neill's Plays Printed Abroad," *College English,* V (March, 1944), 341.
5. Frederic I. Carpenter, "The Romantic Tragedy of Eugene O'Neill," *College English,* VI (February, 1945), 250-58.

Chapter Three

1. See Cargill, *O'Neill,* p. 143.
2. See Richard Dana Skinner, *Eugene O'Neill: The Poet's Quest* (New York, 1935), p. viii.
3. See Engel.
4. The New York *Times,* December 12, 1921.
5. Engel, p. 95.

Chapter Four

1. Gelb, p. 503.
2. Gelb, p. 535.
3. Philip Weissman, "Conscious and Unconscious Autobiographical Dramas of Eugene O'Neill," *Journal of the American Psychoanalytic Association,* V (July, 1957), 432-60.
4. Engel, p. 132.
5. Sophus K. Winther, *"Desire Under the Elms:* A Modern Tragedy," *Modern Drama,* III (December, 1960), 326-32.

Chapter Five

1. See Engel, p. 178.
2. See Engel, pp. 179-80.
3. Doris Alexander, *"Lazarus Laughed* and Buddha," *Modern Language Quarterly,* XVII (December, 1956), 357-65.
4. Walter Kerr, "O'Neill's *Strange Interlude;"* reprinted in Los Angeles *Times,* Calendar, April 7, 1963.

5. Doris Alexander, "*Strange Interlude* and Schopenhauer," *American Literature*, XXV (1953), 213-28.

6. From a letter to F. I. Carpenter, June 24, 1932.

Chapter Six

1. From a letter to F. I. Carpenter, March 24, 1945.

2. See Gelb, p. 762, *passim*.

3. *Ibid.*, p. 777.

4. O'Neill's plan for "the Cycle" has been outlined in Doris Falk, *Eugene O'Neill*, pp. 205-6.

5. Hamilton Basso, "The Tragic Sense," *New Yorker*, XXIV (March 13, 1948), 37-40.

6. Gelb, p. 804.

7. Lee Simonson, *The Stage Is Set* (New York, 1932); reprinted in Cargill, pp. 454-59.

8. Falk, pp. 144-55; reprinted in Cargill, pp. 415-23.

9. Barrett H. Clark, *Eugene O'Neill* (New York, 1947), pp. 143-44.

10. Henry Hewes, "*A Touch of the Poet*," in *Saturday Review of Literature*, April 13, 1957. Reprinted in Cargill, pp. 221-23.

Chapter Seven

1. See Alexander, *passim*.

2. See Engel.

3. Falk, p. 163.

4. Helen Muchnic, "Circe's Swine: Plays by Gorky and O'Neill," reprinted in Cargill, from *Comparative Literature*, III (Spring, 1951), 119-28; and Vivian Hopkins, "*The Iceman* seen through *The Lower Depths*," *College English*, XI (November, 1949), 81-87.

5. Stephen Whicher, "O'Neill's Long Journey," *Commonweal*, LXIII (March 16, 1956), 614-15.

6. *Ibid.*

7. Sophus Winther, "O'Neill's Tragic Themes," *Arizona Quarterly*, XIII (Winter, 1957), 295-307.

8. Mary McCarthy, "A Moon for the Misbegotten," The New York *Times*, August 31, 1952. Reprinted in Cargill.

Chapter Eight

1. The London *Times Literary Supplement* (April 10, 1948). Reprinted in Cargill, p. 369.

2. Eric Bentley, *In Search of Theatre* (New York, 1952). Reprinted in Cargill, pp. 331-45.

3. Francis Fergusson, "Eugene O'Neill," *Hound and Horn* (January, 1930). Reprinted in Cargill, pp. 271-82.

4. Camillo Pellizzi, *English Drama: The Last Great Phase* (London, 1935). Reprinted in Cargill, pp. 353-57.

5. Bernard DeVoto, *Minority Report* (Boston, 1943). Reprinted in Cargill, pp. 301-6.

6. From a letter to the writer, by Professor Anant N. Bhatt, Dharmendrasinhji College, Rajkot, India.

7. Mary B. Mullett, "The Extraordinary Story of Eugene O'Neill," *American Magazine*, XCIV (November, 1922), p. 34.

8. Letter to George Jean Nathan, May 7, 1923.

9. From *The American Spectator* (January, 1933). Reprinted in Cargill, pp. 121-22.

10. From interview by Mullett (note 7).

11. From interview with Oliver M. Sayler, *Century Magazine*, January, 1922. Reprinted in Cargill, p. 107.

Selected Bibliography

The O'Neill bibliography is immense. The following bibliography of primary sources includes only collections of plays by O'Neill published in book form before 1951, and single plays published in book form after 1951. A check list of all O'Neill's completed plays (some of them unpublished) follows, numbering the individual plays in their approximate order of composition.

Similarly, the bibliography of secondary sources, discussing O'Neill and his works, includes only books. The most valuable periodical articles may be found listed in Notes and References.

PRIMARY SOURCES

Thirst, and Other One-Act Plays. Boston, The Gorham Press, 1914. (Includes: *Thirst, The Web, Warnings, Fog,* and *Recklessness.* Limited to 1000 copies. Rare now.)

The Lost Plays of Eugene O'Neill. New York, New Fathoms Press, 1950. (Includes: *Abortion, The Movie Man, The Sniper, Servitude,* and *A Wife for a Life.* A collection of apprentice pieces, forgotten by O'Neill. Minor.)

The Plays of Eugene O'Neill. New York, Random House, 1951. (Three volumes. The standard edition of all O'Neill's important plays published before 1951. Volume I includes: *Strange Interlude, Desire Under the Elms, Lazarus Laughed, The Fountain,* four plays of the sea [*S. S. Glencairn*], *Ile, Where the Cross Is Made, The Rope, The Dreamy Kid, Before Breakfast.* Volume II: *Mourning Becomes Electra, Ah, Wilderness!, All God's Chillun Got Wings, Marco Millions, Welded, Diff'rent, The First Man, Gold.* Volume III: *Anna Christie, Beyond the Horizon, The Emperor Jones, The Hairy Ape, The Great God Brown, The Straw, Dynamo, Days Without End, The Iceman Cometh.*)

A Moon for the Misbegotten. New York, Random House, 1952.

Long Day's Journey Into Night. New Haven, Yale University Press, 1956.

A Touch of the Poet. New Haven, Yale University Press, 1957.

Hughie. New Haven, Yale University Press. 1959.

More Stately Mansions. New Haven, Yale University Press, 1964.

CHECK LIST OF O'NEILL'S COMPLETED PLAYS (In order of approximate date of composition):

1. *A Wife for a Life,* 1913, published 1950, not produced.
2. *Thirst,* 1913, published 1914, produced 1916.
3. *The Web,* 1913, published 1914, not produced.
4. *Warnings,* 1913, published 1914, not produced.

Selected Bibliography

5. *Fog*, 1913, published 1914, produced 1916.
6. *Recklessness*, 1913, published 1914, not produced.
7. *Bound East for Cardiff*, 1914, published and produced 1916.
8. *Servitude*, 1914, published 1950, not produced.
9. *Abortion*, 1914, published 1950, not produced.
10. *The Sniper*, 1915, produced 1917, published 1950.
11. *Before Breakfast*, 1916, produced and published 1916.
12. *The Movie Man*, 1916, published 1950, not produced.
13. *Ile*, 1916, produced 1917, published 1918.
14. *In the Zone*, 1916, produced 1917, published 1919.
15. *The Long Voyage Home*, 1916, produced and published 1917.
16. *The Moon of the Caribbees*, 1916, produced and published 1918.
17. *The Rope*, 1918, produced 1918, published 1919.
18. *The Dreamy Kid*, 1918, produced 1919, published 1920.
19. *Beyond the Horizon*, 1918, produced and published 1920.
20. *Where the Cross Is Made*, 1918, produced 1918, published 1919.
21. *Chris Christopherson*, 1919, produced 1920, not published.
22. *The Straw*, 1919, produced and published 1921.
23. *Exorcism*, 1919, produced 1920, not published.
24. *Gold*, 1920, produced and published 1921.
25. *Anna Christie*, 1920, produced 1921, published 1922.
26. *The Emperor Jones*, 1920, produced 1920, published 1921.
27. *Diff'rent*, 1920, produced 1920, published 1921.
28. *The First Man*, 1921, produced and published 1922.
29. *The Hairy Ape*, 1921, produced and published 1922.
30. *The Fountain*, 1921, produced 1925, published 1926.
31. *Welded*, 1922, produced and published 1924.
32. *The Ancient Mariner*, 1923, produced 1924, published 1960.
33. *All God's Chillun Got Wings*, 1923, produced and published 1924.
34. *Desire Under the Elms*, 1924, produced and published 1924.
35. *Marco Millions*, 1924, published 1927, produced 1928.
36. *The Great God Brown*, 1925, produced and published 1926.
37. *Lazarus Laughed*, 1925, published 1927, produced 1928.
38. *Strange Interlude*, 1926, produced and published 1928.
39. *Dynamo*, 1928, produced and published 1929.
40. *Mourning Becomes Electra*, 1929, produced and published 1931.
41. *Ah, Wilderness!*, 1932, produced and published 1933.
42. *Days Without End*, 1932, produced and published 1934.
43. *A Touch of the Poet*, 1935-1939, published and produced 1957.
44. *More Stately Mansions*, 1936-1939, produced 1962, published 1964.
45. *The Iceman Cometh*, 1939, produced and published 1946.
46. *Long Day's Journey Into Night*, 1940, produced and published 1956.
47. *Hughie*, 1941, produced 1958, published 1959.
48. *A Moon for the Misbegotten*, 1942, produced 1947, published 1952.

SECONDARY SOURCES

A. *Source Book and Bibliographies*

CARGILL, OSCAR, FAGIN, N. B. and FISHER, W. J., editors. *O'Neill and his Plays: Four Decades of Criticism.* New York: New York University Press, 1961. A valuable combination of source book and bibliographical guide. It reprints many important letters and "Off-Stage Observations" by O'Neill, selected reviews of his individual plays, and many of the best articles about him. Its "Appendices" summarize the facts concerning the composition, production and publication of his plays. The "Selected Bibliography" includes about 400 entries.

MILLER, JORDAN Y. *Eugene O'Neill and the American Critic: A Summary and Bibliographical Checklist.* Hamden, Conn.: Archon Books, 1962. The most complete bibliography of books and articles about O'Neill published before 1960, including the most important reviews of his plays. More than 1800 entries.

SANBORN, RALPH, and CLARK, BARRETT H. *A Bibliography of the Works of Eugene O'Neill.* New York: Random House, 1931. Complete information on works by O'Neill to 1931. Not complete on works about O'Neill.

B. *Books of Biography and Criticism in English.*

ALEXANDER, DORIS. *The Tempering of Eugene O'Neill.* New York: Harcourt, Brace and World, 1962. Good biography of O'Neill to 1920. Not so inclusive as the Gelbs's, but full of unique information concerning his parents and early friends. For valuable articles by Professor Alexander discussing the plays, see Cargill, "Bibliography."

BOULTON, AGNES. *Part of a Long Story.* New York: Doubleday, 1958. Reminiscences by O'Neill's second wife concerning their years together, especially 1917 to 1919; frankly personal.

BOWEN, CROSWELL. *The Curse of the Misbegotten: A Tale of the House House of O'Neill.* New York: McGraw, Hill, 1959. Written "with the assistance of Shane O'Neill." Interesting, but uncritical in using information from Shane and his mother, Agnes. Some doubtful hypotheses stated as facts.

CLARK, BARRETT H. *Eugene O'Neill: The Man and His Plays.* New York: Dover Publications, 1947. The last edition of the first book about O'Neill, first published in 1926. Contains much valuable information supplied by O'Neill, and letters and interviews.

ENGEL, EDWIN A. *The Haunted Heroes of Eugene O'Neill.* Cambridge, Mass.: Harvard University Press, 1953. A well-written, often negative, critical study of O'Neill's individual plays, and of his development as dramatist.

FALK, DORIS V. *Eugene O'Neill and the Tragic Tension: An Interpretative Study of the Plays.* New Brunswick, New Jersey: Rutgers University Press, 1958. A thoughtful interpretation, combining psychological with literary criticism.

Selected Bibliography

GASSNER, JOHN, editor. *O'Neill: A Collection of Critical Essays.* Englewood Cliffs, New Jersey: Prentice-Hall, 1964. A well-chosen collection of essays about O'Neill, some of them previously unpublished.

GELB, ARTHUR and BARBARA. *O'Neill.* New York: Harper and Brothers, 1962. The most complete biography of O'Neill, and (with Doris Alexander's) the best yet published. Particularly valuable for personal interviews and reminiscences of O'Neill's many friends and associates. Not documented.

LEECH, CLIFFORD. *Eugene O'Neill.* New York, Grove Press, Inc., 1963. Good, brief introduction by a British critic.

MICKLE, ALAN D. *Six Plays of Eugene O'Neill.* New York: Liveright, 1929. An early appreciation by an Australian who had never seen an O'Neill play produced. Overenthusiastic.

SKINNER, RICHARD DANA. *Eugene O'Neill: A Poet's Quest.* New York: Longmans, Green, 1935. Sympathetic interpretation from the Catholic point of view.

WINTHER, SOPHUS KEITH. *Eugene O'Neill: A Critical Study.* New York: Random House, 1934. Second edition, enlarged, Russell and Russell, 1961. An interpretation of O'Neill's "Dominant Ideas," with little discussion of the plays individually. Professor Winther has published valuable interpretations of the individual plays in periodicals (see Cargill, "Bibliography").

Books devoted to O'Neill and his plays have been published in four foreign languages: French, Spanish, German, and Swedish. A recent book by Leon Mirlas (Buenos Aires, 1961) contains important letters of O'Neill. Professor Horst Frenz has published many articles documenting the publication and production of O'Neill's plays abroad (see Cargill, "Bibliography").

Index

Index